MW01468850

LIFE IS SHORT AND IS AN ADVENTURE

WHEN FATE KNOCKS YOU DOWN, LOOK TO GOD AND CONTINUE WITH YOUR LIFE: A MEMOIR

TIM V. MCGUIRK

DORRANCE PUBLISHING CO
EST. 1920
PITTSBURGH, PENNSYLVANIA 15238

Dorrance Publishing Co
585 Alpha Drive
Pittsburgh, PA 15238
Visit our website at *www.dorrancebookstore.com*

ISBN: 979-8-88925-118-7
eISBN: 979-8-88925-618-2

All of a Sudden, it's 8:00 o'clock pm...
... It's bedtime when you're little.
Chasing fireflies as a kid.

I will pick you up for a date at 8:00.
8 o'clock - it's when dinner is over -
the dishes are done - family time.

And it's bedtime again when you are old.
All of a sudden, it's 8 o'clock...
a lifetime of memories.

THE TWENTY THIRD PSALM

A psalm of David:
The Lord is my shepherd: I shall not want.
He makes me to lie down in green pastures,
He leads me beside the still waters.
He restores my soul.
He guides me in straight paths for His Name's sake.
Yea, though I walk through the valley of the shadow of death,
I will fear no evil
For Thou art with me.
Thy rod and Thy staff, they comfort me.
Thou preparest a table before me in the presence of mine
enemies.
Thou anointest my head with oil,
My cup runneth over.
Surely goodness and mercy shall follow me all the days of
my life,
And I shall dwell in the House of the Lord forever.

✦

A **memoir** (from <u>French</u>: *mémoire*: *memoria*, meaning *memory* or *reminiscence*) is a collection of memories that an individual writes about moments or events, both public or private, that took place in the subject's life. The assertions made in the work are understood to be factual. While memoir has historically been defined as a subcategory **of biography or autobiography since the late twentieth century**, presenting a narrowed focus. A biography or autobiography tells the story "of a life", while a memoir often tells "a story from a life", such as events and turning points from the author's life. The author of a memoir may be referred to as a *memoirist* or a *memorialist*.

INTRODUCTION

We have all had those times in life when suddenly we are dealt a painful blow. It's a shock, and it hurts, and it knocks us off balance; we struggle to stay on our feet, but sometimes we fall. This is my life story of the punches I've taken, some violent, like serious injury or sickness or disability, a freak accident, a betrayal, other times loneliness as when we realize how disconnected we are from others. And the short, sharp shocks when we catch our reflection, and we don't like what we see. Those painful stabs of failure, disappointment, and rejection.

I did not write this book to teach any lessons but to demonstrate how I survived and maybe some readers will gain third-hand experience from my exposure. I hope these tales will open up your heart and your mind, and the stories are designed to be lighthearted when necessary and damn serious where they need be. And I hope you enjoy the journey and remember that life dealt me several blows, but I managed to always get back up.

This memoir is mainly aimed at my grandchildren. So they can know who their grandfather was and the stories that made up his life.

I hardly knew my grandparents and the ways in which they took on the trials and tribulations of life, their stories of successes and failures, where they lived and how. And these blind spots in family histories bothered me, and still do. Who died from what sickness and at what age?

I knew my paternal grandfather more than any of my grandparents. My grandmother died when I was six months old, and my grandfather remarried later in life to a lady named Ruth. They lived on forty acres of ground outside of Salem, Missouri, as long as I can remember and had an out-door toilet which we kids always thought of as a novelty.

My grandfather was a wiry old man full of life and always kept himself busy whistling. He had an old horse; my cousin Larry and I once literally scared the shit out of with an air rifle, and the old horse kept my grandfather busy.

I remember going to my grandpa's place was a lot of fun because I got to see all my cousins, Uncles, and Aunts.

Maybe that's part of the reason I'm writing, to share with my grandchildren what a wonderful group of people I grew up with and some of their stories and our interactions.

On my mother's side, I had only visited my grandfather twice, once when I was about ten years old at the supper table and once in 1969 when he was on his death bed and my mother went to be with him.

My maternal grandmother was more French than English growing up in Quebec, Canada, and her background I can say now is a blank, with a few exceptions I should write about for family knowledge and medical historical note.

I'm writing this book as an informative note concerning the traumas and illnesses I have suffered throughout life. Yes, I've had my share and then some of life's knockdowns and some problems and dimensions I've had to live with are inherited.

The traumas I have suffered I'll write about as we go forward since most have followed me throughout my life in seemingly ascending years, but the medical illnesses, well hell, they still follow me and have been since I was born.

I have been having fun despite the insufferable problems mainly because of the people I've met in this life. Some were good folks, some were true friends, some were hilarious and not meaning to be, many I miss, and then I've run into my share of troublemakers.

My story is a story of both faith and luck, and it is a story of never giving up with disappointment after trauma after failure, but somehow, I was always being pulled up and getting up again and again and lurching forward. Through the grace of God, luck of the Irish and pure determination, I hope to set an example for my grandchildren. Life is short and enjoyable.

TABLE OF CONTENTS

IN THE BEGINNING

Most of my earliest memories come from family; parents before they passed away, my Aunts and Uncles, and my older sister, God bless her soul, and at times I believe she's still trying to give me advice. But most of it is not sinking in.

Although that may suggest that some of my writing in this memoir is second-hand, I have been diligent in creating my narratives as factual as possible using the memories of what I have experienced.

I was born in Austin, Texas in 1952, my Mother twenty-one years at the time and my Father was thirty years, (the nine years difference in my parent's ages was explained to us kids because Mom said, my Father was so young looking when they were dating she did not think of him being that much older than her). Sure mom. He was a handsome American soldier, period.

My older sister was born in 1950; Janet Marlene and so began this family of army brats. As the years went by, I had a sister Bridget, a sister Frances, and a sister Carolyn.

As an army family, we moved almost every other year and a half or every two years depending on my father's assignments. I started first grade at Salem Elementary school, because the family was left in Salem, Missouri, while my dad was stationed overseas.

I can still remember hating first grade and one reason was because I had to walk to and from school with my sister and my Uncle John, a most impatient leader who was fourteen years at the time. Neither cared how far ahead of me they were while we were walking to and fro, and this made me half cry and always struggle to catch up.

In school, I was afraid of the rowdy kids and so I stayed close to my sister. She would complain to my mother that I pestered her at recess and lunch because I would not play with the other kids. Eating the white paste at school was the most fun I remember having and when the bell rang, I ran looking for my sister. But that's about all I remember about Salem Elementary because before long we, as a family, moved to my father's next station base, Worms, Germany.

Soon we were on our way to Worms, Germany as my dad was given orders to bring his family with him on this assignment because this time, he would be stationed for three years as a generator technician for anti-aircraft missile projects.

In Germany, I went to base school and got along quite well with the kids, making many friends and several; Lee Lescher, Bill Mason, and Eddie Zorrow, I still remember as fellow cub scouts. We were buddies at school and at base housing.

Base housing consisted of four-story apartment buildings and a soldier's rank determined what floor you lived on, we were on the first floor, my dad was a master sergeant.

Learning a little German helped us get along in the German confection stores we kids were always visiting and we knew the German money system quite well. My mother taught us how not to be cheated out of correct change.We bought many things from the German confection stores but mainly biscuits and other bread stuffs. The German stores and neighborhoods were across the street from the American housing apartments and were behind walls of trees and hedges as if being fenced off, but we kids just bypassed all the natural blockades and headed for the stores.

The German kids were nice enough although skirmishes broke out during times of soccer play between us, but then the game would end and the German kids would quit the game and head home yelling, "dumbkoff, sheitzkoff, swine," and so on at us if we came even close to scoring.

The American housing units were situated in a square so there would be a big park like area in the center of the apartment buildings. This area is where we played. The German kids would now and then take over this area for themselves since where they lived it was house against house and no play areas. But for the most part we all got along, the German and American kids.

My father enjoyed touring Germany, and every now and then we would all pile into the 1956 Bel Air my father had shipped from the states, and we'd hit the autobahns. We'd visit everything from Heidelberg Castle to the Church in the Rocks, but being so young a kid, it didn't mean that much to see such historic sites and so I don't remember enough to write about these wonders except for their names. We went to all types of festivals, real Oktoberfest celebrations and sometimes we'd embark on picnicking near the Rhine River, although the German people would swim in parts of the river, we American personnel were prohibited by general orders from swimming in the Rhine.

I traveled with my father to his base location several times without my sisters to see the generators he worked on that he explained were necessary to keep the missile installations lit up in case of Russian attack. As kids, we were aware of the dreaded Russians. We were taught both at school and at home how evil they were and I was proud of my dad for being a soldier keeping the wicked Russians away. My mind was in wonder at the size and noise the generators made, and I never missed a chance to go see the monstrosities, while my father I guess just wanted to buddy up with his only surviving son at the time.

We kids had a sort of entertainment at home too. We read and collected comic books and records. German television left a lot to be desired, even the cartoons were in German, and you had to be really bored and it had to be nasty weather outside to get you to watch German TV. Comic books and records were plentiful at the PX, and my parents allowed us to earn money for both… although it always seemed I had to "police the area" twice as often as my sisters to earn any money for my things.

German winters were filled with snow and American sleds were of little value for playing with. We all turned to the deep rudder German sleds with no steering power, which made for some hair-raising fun going downhill. I remember pulling my little sisters in one of the German type sleds we had. We brought one home with us and when spotted by American kids in the states, our German sled was a sure curiosity item.

The family got orders to head back to the 'states' after three years. My mother happened to be having a baby in a few months and she wanted to get back to the states before the baby was born, I remember her telling us. Several weeks later, we said our goodbyes to our friends and off we went.

Flying in the plane was fun but noisy. It was prop driven, and we could see the ground for most of the flight over Germany and France. My dad tried to point out where we might be flying over. Before memory could serve up much distance, we landed in New York City. We only spent a couple of nights in New York, and it wasn't long before we piled back into the old Bel Air. Later, my mother told me we were waiting for the car to arrive in New York so we could move on to our next destination, El Paso, Texas. It took days, I remember, to get to the mountains and desert of El Paso, but no sooner did we find an unfurnished house to bed down in, then along came my sister Carolyn.

I remember sleeping on mattresses on the floor and one day my sister Janet and Bridget, and I welcomed home my mom and dad at what was then home with a new baby. She got to the new home before our furniture did.

As kids, we always wanted a pet. Preferably a dog, but we didn't know the difference between having a puppy or a full-grown dog. I remember clearly one day my dad brought home from base a stray mutt the size of a retriever, a dog/pet for us kids. We were so excited. But first my dad told us we had to clean him up. So, we got the garden hose, a washtub, and some bath soap and we spent a whole lot of time getting wet with our pup, washing him down. After we dried him, Janet, Bridget, Frances, and I dried him good…

Then my dad told us we had to pick the ticks off him. What were ticks? My dad got a metal trash can, poured some Zippo lighter fluid in the bottom of it, and showed us how he pulled these bugs off our doggie, especially around his ears, and put the bugs in the bottom of the trash can. We all yelled in horror at the sight of these bugs and to see them wiggling in the can, but my dad knew what he was doing and moved fast and told us to keep back. When he was done picking off the bugs, he threw a match into the trash bucket and burned up all the nasty bugs. From that day on, I've always associated ticks with lighter fluid.

My dad explained the bugs were blood suckers and had hooked on to our new dog and had to be picked off and burned up, otherwise they would carry germs. This was the time before flea and tick collars and your pet had to be hand groomed if it had a chance against fleas and ticks. My dad was a specialist.

We next built our "best in show" a doghouse and painted it.

CALL FOR THE BALL...

El Paso, Texas was a fine place to live and play and as kids we were constantly with friends. The weather was always warm, and the occasional rainstorm gave us the chance to play in the rain. We lived at first in a small home on the outskirts of base, but soon moved into a subdivision of lookalike homes with yards, a far cry from the apartment complexes of Germany.

School was a lot of fun because there were so many kids. We went to school with a mixture of army brats and public kids, that's what we called ourselves. A lot of our friends were Mexican American, but we never knew a difference, and no one ever noticed. Our school was made up of several large buildings and when the bell rang, we went to different classrooms, but recess and lunch break is what we lived for. Our play area was an open ground desert with the shrub cut out and this made for some fine ball fields and soccer fields.

I was a short round kid and soccer didn't interest me, but I was surely into baseball, with the old man being a St. Louis Cardinals Fan, and that rubbed off onto me. I was built right to be a catcher. Every second we had time to play ball, the other kids smart enough to know not to get behind the plate, would yell that, "McGuirk is catcher!" And the only protective gear the school had was a catcher's mask. I was eleven years old.

This one lunch period came while I was catching, and the pitcher threw the ball and the batter hit the ball straight up between the pitcher's mound and home plate. I remember jumping up, throwing off my catcher's mask so I could see the ball and went charging to get under it.

The next thing I knew I was laying on the ground... *BLOOD ALL OVER THE SIDE OF MY FACE... The pitcher ran up towards the school screaming and two kids panickily tried to help me get to my feet.*

Evidently the pitcher and I had... COLLIDED HEAD ON... over trying to catch the pop up, but that I didn't know that fact until my dad explained what had happened several days later and then chastised me for not "calling for the ball".

I got to my feet, STILL BLEEDING… and my helpers were now YELLING for someone to get the nurse while I was being led to the school buildings. Finally, at the nurses' station, I remember the nurse and several teachers were aiding me and the pitching kid who was still screaming. I had not made a sound throughout the entire time and then I was handed a towel and told to wipe my face.

After wiping my face, I remember ALL THE BLOOD ALL OVER THE TOWEL, and I began to ask if I was dying. Now I understand I had suffered a BIG GASHED HEAD WOUND, and head wounds bleed, along with a BUSTED NOSE, but back then to me it was life threatening, whatever happened. I still had only a head injury, but I remember a headache. Everyone was asking me how bad I was hurting, but all I could come up with was a headache.

I was BLEEDING IN THE NURSE'S OFFICE FOREVER it seemed when my dad came in wearing his workday fatigues and rushed over to me as if he had seen a ghost. I had a headache, a bloody towel, bloody shirt, and the blood had just been cleaned off my face and when I saw him, my panic set in. My dad helped me up and away we went to the Bel Air and flew to the emergency room of Beaumont Hospital.

I was holding the same towel over my head when a nurse came up to me and told me to pull it away so she could see the wound. When I did, she turned different colors it seemed and called for a doctor. Again, no crying or protesting on my part, I remember just... **BEING SCARED.**

The bleeding had stopped, but later I discovered that I had a swelling the size of a large egg right over my right temple, a very dangerous wound. The doctor told them to stitch me up and then he got on the phone. I can vividly remember everything in the hospital as if it was a slow-motion movie. I walked into a room. They cleaned me up some more, told me to prepare for the sting of the alcohol on my head, and away the shears went, cutting my hair.

The next thing I knew, I had stitches and a terrific headache which by now two doctors asked me to describe. My first ride in a wheelchair was to an X-ray where they turned my sore head every which way and sent me back to my dad in the waiting room. He was still white colored and serious looking. After some time, a doctor came into the area and sat down with my dad and I and told us I had *a fracture in my skull next to my temple.*

(A side note: In 2014, I fell backwards down some steps at home and landed on my head, and was taken to St. Clare Hospital in Fenton, Missouri. They performed an MRI on my head, and it came back negative except the doctor explained I had a fracture scar ON my right temple. She asked how such a fracture occurred and after I told her, she explained such a wound is usually very serious, especially over the temple. Presently she explained my fall resulted in a mild concussion and transferred me out of radiology.)

The Beaumont Hospital attending doctor continued talking to my dad and I and explained the swelling we all see is either blood leaking through the fracture or the tissue surrounding the area caused by the "trauma." (The first time I would remember that word). They wanted me to stay at the hospital a few hours to see if the swelling grows in size (real modern medicine), and they wanted me to stay in a room, but I said, "No way, I'm going home." The first time in my life I stood up for myself and I was only eleven years old.

They sent me home with instructions to keep calm, the damn hospital was scary and noisy with sick people, doctors, pain; home was Mom, sisters, and television with food.

Once home, Mom was crying so then I started crying, my sisters were crying. Janet stood stalwart and just wanted to look at my head. I missed a few days of school because of the reoccurring headaches and my dad took me back to the hospital. They ran an *electroencephalographer on my head and chest to try and discover any damage inside that might be causing the headaches, but everything came back negative*. Wonderful. The doctor explained that the headaches were a result of my injury, and they would soon stop bothering me. He was right. After several weeks, the headaches subsided, and I tried to get back to my old self. But I never did. My headaches to this day start on my right side for whatever reason.

HORNED TOADS AND TUMBLE WEEDS

One of the finer sports we desert kids took part in was catching, or trying to catch as far as a round kid could (called "husky" in the jeans department at Sears and Roebuck), tumble weeds and horned toads. I always had problems with the gang when it came running down my share of tumble weeds. We used old brooms to stab 'em, and the other kids said "McGuirk is just slow because he's fat!" But anyway, it was the sport of the hunt that counted. We'd pile the weeds up against a fence level and pretend we had a fort. It worked well until we got bored and then we'd tear it all down.

Horned toad arenas were built of wet sand circles, catch a gray (harmless) horned toad and keep him in the arena with several sticks. Then get some black ants to crawl up on some loose-leaf school paper and pop them into the arena. Then root for the toad to eat the ants before they escaped. And kids today with their electronics and computer games don't know what they're missing.

The semi-desert of El Paso made for great playground territory and kids made the best of it. I'm glad I got a chance to live in El Paso.

SALEM, MISSOURI

After fourteen months in El Paso, my father was given orders to ship back to Worms, Germany, but this time without the family. So, we headed to live in Salem, Missouri, the place where my father had family that could help us get by.

We left El Paso, all seven of us in the Bel Air, and pointed towards the Midwest. Somehow my parents kept us together on the trajectory we had to take and several gas station bathrooms later, and, for me, several times opening the car door on the side of the road later, we made it to Salem.

The car pulled into Uncle Jim's, and Aunt Mary's place and we were never so happy to see these folks as we were at that time. *(Side note: I capitalize all "Uncle" and "Aunt" notations throughout this book because of my utmost respect, admiration, and reverence for these people of my family.)*

No more Bel Air car for a while. No more backseat bologna sandwiches, and no more crying little sisters. No more gas station bathroom service. Friendly, smiling, welcoming faces... cousins our size and age. A house, although a little one, a house and a yard with grass and trees.

After all the hugs and hellos, we went inside the house and filled it righteously. I, at first, was introduced to my cousin Ronnie's GI Joe collection. I was a bit taken aback. These were dolls. Actually the first action figures, but dolls to me and I tried working all the arms and legs and couldn't believe my eyes that dolls for boys were such a toy. My sisters were impressed at the same time, sitting next to me with my cousin Linda's Barbie doll collection. I think that among my sisters, they had two Barbie dolls total. What a great bunch of toys Linda and Ronnie had.

We were next invited into the kitchen for sandwiches, it was getting dark, and I remember my Aunt Mary fixing floor pallets for us kids while we were eating sandwiches, and because there was nowhere to sit, I was standing next to my dad as he was explaining his near future family plan to Uncle Jim. Since Mom couldn't drive and there were five of us kids, staying near family such as the relatives in Salem was a must, and of course I remember Uncle Jim's serious expression agreeing. This meant we were now Salemites.

It was hard to believe the number of trophies my Uncle Jim had displayed on a mantle in the living room. I stared for the longest time. And Uncle Jim was as proud as punch of the trophies, explaining what they were for, pitching and bowling. Ronnie showed me his trophies but that just made me jealous.

The adults stayed up for the longest time, but we kids passed out after my little sisters finished doing some crying and fussing. The floor was better than trying to sleep over the hump on the car's back floor.

Aunt Mary woke us up with a breakfast call and I remember the first morning in Salem very well. Soon Ronnie showed me his bike and apple tree which Uncle Jim yelled at us not to eat from, this green crab apple tree. Uncle Jim then gave my dad a tour of his vegetable garden and I tagged along to see what growing vegetables looked like.

It wasn't long before a car pulled up in the gravelly driveway and out jumped my cousin Larry and then came my Uncle Tony and Aunt Avella with little Susie. Relatives I didn't remember, but was happy to meet. We played horseshoes and Ronnie and Larry showed me Ronnie's fishing gear, which I never knew existed. I mean what was a rod and reel?

Before long, we were all headed for Grandpa McGuirk's place on the outskirts of town…it took about a half hour to get there, and all the latter part of the trip was on a gravel road. Cool. We pulled up with Uncle Jim and Uncle Tony in line on the grass lot in front of the house. A farmhouse, a barn, and what turned out to be an outhouse. Cool again.

I didn't remember my grandfather, and when his wife came to meet us, none of us knew her. Ruth was her name, but we kids were raised that everyone was titled so we called her Grandmother Ruth.

Of course, one of my little sisters had to be the first one to use the outhouse and Grandpa went and cleaned it up in a hurry. I soon found out what cleaning it up meant… shooing and swatting away the bugs! You did your business quick and got out and I always had someone like Larry or Ronnie on the outside laughing the whole time I was using the place.

This place was what a forest and woods were all about. A pond, a bed spring chained between two trees for swinging, a flat cut area for a softball field, slightly overgrown at times, some kind of tank later to be discovered for LP gas, and Ruth had birdhouses all over the place.

(Side note: My cousin and I one time went out to Grandpa's with our dads who were doing whatever and Larry and I had firecrackers. We thought it would be cool to scare the shit out of some birds by putting some lit firecrackers in this big, beautiful birdhouse of Ruth's. We weren't old enough to be smart but old enough to be stupid, so we threw about four Red Balls into the house, with long wicks. Hid. And KABOOM! The entire birdhouse disappeared! We ran like hell for the cars, got in, and hid on the floor, too scared to laugh. But evidently no one was around to hear or see what we had done, and we got away with it...)

Grandpa's place was great for nighttime parties. Everybody in the family would show up as if it was a special holiday. The wood would be placed in the huge fireplace in the yard, and everyone would anticipate who would drive up to the house next. I was with every cousin I could find and then I noticed my cousin Bridget Ann for the first time. That's all they wrote. I was no longer interested in firecrackers, boy cousins, daylight, or oxygen.

Uncle Harry drove up in a yellow and white Lincoln Continental and out popped Anthony and Rose. Two cousins I didn't know I had until then. Aunt Theresa got out of the car yelling at Uncle Harry to open the trunk.

Uncle Tom I didn't know at all and at one party I remember he and I were crossing paths to the outhouse when he stopped mid-stride and looked at me kind of funny. I thought he was trying to guess my name, so I said, "I'm Timmy, Vince's kid." Uncle Tom just stared, didn't say a word, and fell flat on his face in front of me. I looked down at him in shock as he groaned, then I went running to get help. Too many beers.

Grandpa was great with a harmonica and after a couple of beers he could play up a storm. Some would dance, others tried to sing, but no one stayed still. We roasted hot dogs and whatever anyone brought to grill over an open fire. There'd be thirty or more people at the party.

In due time, Uncle John built Grandpa an indoor bathroom and then he built a small cabin building about 100 feet from the house where the boys could drink and play cards. I remember the little clubhouse as a lot of fun.

One day when I was about nineteen years old, we had a party out at Grandpa's and we men all gathered at the little clubhouse building talking and telling jokes, when my Uncle Joe McGuirk asked everyone, "Where's Danny (my older first cousin)?" No one knew. I told my dad I was going up to the house. It was dark, and I had a hard time walking in the dark with my bad legs. He agreed and off I went through the knee-high weeds to the house. When all of a sudden, I stepped down on a person lying on the ground and we both let out a yell. I lost my balance and hit the ground. The person I stepped on sat up laughing. It was Danny with his girlfriend making woo in the tall grass. He asked me if I was okay, and I said sure, except I shit in my pants from fright!

Grandpa had forty acres of ground and two squirrels and three deer are all that lived on that acreage. I know because I went squirrel hunting and deer hunting with Uncle John on a couple of occasions. And the lonely rabbit that lived there was smart as hell. When we went deer hunting, Uncle John and I did everything right. He got up in a tree and I buried myself in the brush. But no luck. So, we drank coffee and Reindeer wine to celebrate the expedition.

DIVISION STREET

We had a good place to live in Salem with plenty of yard and a street that was seldom used, a good street for wagons and bikes. I had a wagon but no bicycle. Mom said we couldn't afford to buy me a bike. What with having to use powdered milk for my four sisters and all living on my dad's allotment checks, a bike was just out of the question.

So, I made do with what was left of a Radio Flyer. One leg in and one leg pedaling, and you could make some headway when necessary. It was tough keeping up with Larry who had a bike and stayed at our house on babysitting duty while his folks worked. Larry told me I was too fat and big to ride his bike so I had no choice but to hope for a better day when I could get a bike.

One of my duties as the male of the family was my weekly trek to Adams Market, about six blocks from home with my wagon to fetch groceries for my mom and sisters. I'd go to the market, hand the grocer a list, and collect the groceries. Sometimes four bags full of goods which meant a slow balancing act back home with an occasional spill now and then. Progress back home was even more tedious during snow or rain, but I must have made the trip fifty times or more…. dang good wagon!

Once in a while, Uncle John would show up at the house to visit and this was always an occasion for celebration… He brought stories of the Navy and what have ya… And one day he came with his newest acquisition, a pink Dodge with tassels in the rear window, what a car. We all got a ride.

Enter Uncle Tony one day. My 1963 birthday… It was put together and everything. Looking better than any new car I have ever owned since. It took me about ten minutes to learn to balance to ride on this magnificence, and I never looked back. I rode everywhere. In fact, I became quite the rider when I challenged a dog or two or more on trips to my cousin's house. Known to be good at standing speed I let nothing stop me on my bike.

Larry lived about a mile and a half from us. I enjoyed going over to his house (I'm sure more than he enjoyed seeing me), and I would ride over to play, but I had to run past a feedlot that contained a pack of bike chasing dogs. I used to psych myself up to make the run every time I decided to visit Larry. After a while, I was told to call before I came over… kinda like I was wearing my welcome thin. I'd hit the road with my tires and pedals in sync on top of "feedlot hill". The run from the dogs was downhill, then a 100 foot straight away and then back uphill for a total of about 300 feet. I could see the little critters, but they weren't paying attention to me at the top of the hill while I was just sitting there. Then BANG… off went the gun in my head and down the hill I'd start at full throttle… standing on the pedals with all my strength… luckily, cars seldom used feedlot road… I watched the pasture for the dogs and halfway down the hill here they came at full gallop and barking their lungs out… The chase was on!

Where the hill leveled out, the dogs squirmed under a fence and caught up with me yapping at my feet and wheels… but I was going as fast as the chain would take me… no more chain… just pure speed and three maybe four yelling mutts… I'd hit he upside of the far hill and the dogs would by now have given up and I'd stand up on the pedal chain combo up the hill and onto flat road to Larry's house. The same scenario would be played back when returning home. I was never bit or knocked over by the dogs… they were just pissed my bike was on their road and meant to let the pedals and wheels know it!

The time spent at my Uncle Tony's place was educational as well as fun. Since there were no trees in El Paso that we as kids could climb, there was a giant black walnut tree in Uncle Tony's backyard that was begging for kids to climb it, but you had to know how. Cousin Larry could climb this tree like a monkey. I just gazed in wonder at the size and height of this tree, hoping someday I'd be able to climb its black and green leafy branches.

Uncle Tony gave me a boost one day and instructed me on where to grab what branch and where to put my feet and before long I was about ten feet up the tree and hanging on for dear life, pretending not to be afraid. I remember staying up in the tree for about twenty minutes and then asking desperately how to get down. Another full set of instructions later, I was close enough to the ground to fall to the ground without any broken bones and happy my first tree climbing attempt was over. But Uncle Tony wasn't done with me yet.

One visit to Larry's came upon the same day he and his dad had gone squirrel hunting the morning before. The two of them had bagged about ten squirrels. Uncle Tony told me it was time I learned how to skin and dress a squirrel. And so began an interesting part of my life. I learned how to skin the squirrel and how two men working together could field dress several squirrels more easily with practice. I will never forget the sounds or smell of the endeavor, nor will I ever forget the taste of the meal the squirrels gave up.

I learned a lot from Uncle Tony. Even how to build model monsters. Larry had a collection of all the model monsters then starring on television: from the Deep Water Thing to Dracula to the Mummy. I forget how many, but they were all built perfectly and painted perfectly. We could not play with them but they sure were neat to look at.

SACRED HEART SCHOOL AND CHURCH

In Salem, you either went to public school or a little Catholic school called Sacred Heart school which was attached to Sacred Heart church. My mother chose to send us to Sacred Heart school which had a total enrollment of thirty-two children grades one through seven. I enjoyed going to school at Sacred Heart. We had five students in my grade and shared the same room with my sister Janet's seventh grade class.

Two nuns taught school, one nun for us fifth, sixth, and seventh graders and one nun for the little kids, which included Bridget and Frances. Because of the intense close supervision of teaching directly from the nuns, we later were discovered to be all advanced in our grades and lessons. But recess and lunch time were the most fun. We boys got together in the school yard and played knights and crusaders. The yard was too small for sports but had enough room for pretend sword fighting and wrestling. It was lots of fun choosing sides with the little kids always going last. Pat Bruger was one knight and Richard Baker the other knight. I was formidable but slow in running and always got slayed easily and quickly.

Sometimes we older boys were given permission to go to the Salem library together and take out a book or two.

We were always on a time limit, and I had to run/walk to try and keep up with Richard Baker and Pa Brugert, but they had no time to wait and would always get there way ahead of me checking out the books. I always went for the old standards, Mark Twain, or cowboy shorts. Fun memories even though Pat and Richard would be back way ahead of me and occasionally Sister Joseph would chastise me for being slow or late, unknowingly because of my now starting to cripple muscular dystrophy.

I became an altar boy. Serving at mass was a big ego booster even though learning the Latin prayers was tricky. Richard Baker was the expert altar boy and Latin prayer man. He tried his best to make a good altar boy out of me, but it was a tough job. The Sister who scheduled the altar boys for masses always put me with Richard. He never complained, and we got the job done, except when I'd make a mistake and then he'd take over and help Father out. And once in a while, my cassock would get stuck on the heel of my shoe while kneeling and I couldn't get up, Richard would come along behind me, undo the bind, and we'd get back at the job. My Uncle Jim would always tease me about these times. Being an altar boy at a funeral was fun, especially on a weekday. I'd be out of school for several hours and the thought of always getting a tip from a funeral director, plus having a special job such as carrying a candle. Funeral duty was a great break for altar boys.

It was about this time I noticed Carol and Diane Wulff... a couple of dolls who went to our school and evidently, I made an impression on Carol who was in my grade. Diane was older and didn't know if I was alive or dead, but Carol was cute and smiled at me a lot. My Uncle Jim knew the family and would take us to their farm every once in a while, and I never missed a trip. On the Wulff farm, they had a few cows and I remember a bull. It was the first time I had ever been close to such big animals. Tom Wulff, the father, also had a barn loaded with hay that we walked through once. It was a magic place for me and my sisters. Carol would play music on her record player in the attic kids' room when it got dark, and we were still visiting. But I had my attention glued on her and her every move. I now can realize one of my first crushes was left behind when my dad decided to move us to St. Louis.

I'll never forget growing up for a couple of years in Salem with Uncle Jim teaching me how to bowl, fish, and how to collect soda bottles for the return money and all of what Uncle Tony taught me and for my bike. Uncle Jim also taught us as kids how to play kick the can. Ronnie was always an expert at the game but boy was it fun playing. Everybody hides, somebody counts to twenty, then everyone runs to see who can kick the can furthest... I think that's how it's played, but maybe I forgot, it's been so long ago. I remember playing at night by the light of the telephone pole streetlight in front of our side yard.

I also want to remember the Uncle Napoleon Bonaparte Wilson I had in Salem with my beloved Aunt Mary Wilson. Uncle Poli, as we all called him, used to run a secondhand farm for Old Man Redman, as we kids understood it. He had several cows and hogs and about four hundred dogs (slight exaggeration), and all of them were in the role of producing or breeding something akin to a population explosion. Uncle Poli was older and didn't care much what his animals did as long as they didn't get mean. We came in when harvest time came for Uncle Poli's garden. He would pay the Landau Cab Company to pick us kids up with our mother and take us the eight miles out of town. He'd show us what was ready for pickin', was they green beans, strawberries, digging up taters, or what have ya... We kids would jump in with both hands. This would happen several times a year and as a reward one –time, Uncle Poli gave us a puppy.

Whenever I get out of purgatory after I die and finish my long walk as all sinners must, I'm sure going to be happy to meet up with my deceased Aunts and Uncles from Salem, who most assuredly are in God's Heaven.

ST. LOUIS

120 miles from Salem and Miss Carol Wulff we landed in the Bel Air in St. Louis, the biggest city I could ever imagine. My dad moved here because he retired from the army and wanted to pursue a civil service job where his army seniority would aid in finding a good job.

We settled at 6721 Michigan Ave. in South St. Louis. A fine neighborhood with a movie show across the street and a public school the size of the Pentagon just a few blocks away. We kids had to transition again to living in an apartment building and this place had no yard. Michigan Avenue was a busy street, and we didn't get over watching the cars for days. Inside was one large room from living room to kitchen with a bathroom in the middle. Oh well, it was now home.

Blow school was bigger than the El Paso school and was hard to take all in at first sight. I remember the classroom I was put in had more kids in it than what seemed the entire enrollment of Sacred Heart school. I never saw Janet once dad dropped us off at the playground which seemed bigger than a farm area. The bathroom had maybe twenty urinals and just as many door-less toilets. The month I went to Blow school, I was just awestruck the whole time by the size of the place, and the number of kids at recess. Whoever put this place together did so for big numbers of kids. I made one friend, his name was Ken, but that's about all I remember about him. My mother delivered us from this place to go to St. Boniface Catholic School a few blocks from home.

At St. Boniface, I again found myself in a big classroom of kids. I sat next to a kid who asked me a lot of questions about myself, and this kid soon found out I was an ace at math during class discussion and whatever went on those first few days. This same kid walked home my way home, north on Michigan, with several other kids. No names were exchanged the first couple of days, we didn't know how to introduce ourselves. About the third day of my turning in perfect scored papers, this kid's name comes to light from the nun who taught us, Roy Esdridge.

(Side note: Roy became my closest friend, a friend I had for thirty-three years, and we were inseparable. I attribute him with helping me grow up, mature, survive, and prosper when I did, pick myself up when life knocked me down, and raise a family properly. He even taught me how to think critically. I enjoyed our friendship through thick and thin, the thin years when he beat me up for getting too smart alecki when we were kids and talking me out of stupid thought when we were older.)

Well, Roy and Jerry Zych and I made up a threesome of pals in seventh grade at school and it was a pretty good friendship with a pecking order not necessary to establish since Roy was a foot taller than Jerry or me. I was supposedly the smart one, Jerry the funny man and goof off, and Roy the born leader. Many times, Jerry would make fun of the way I was walking (unknowing of why), and one time was too many for Roy and Roy punched him. It was the first time in my life that anyone stood up for me and I was taken back, not to mention Jerry was reeled over, and that was the end of the making fun of my walking. Later in life when I was wearing my polio braces Jerry used to, in good fun, ask me if they allowed me to climb telephone poles, fly, and so on…

Before long, I went to Roy's house up the street from where we lived and met his dad.

(Side note: Mr. Esdridge and I became good friends for thirty years, playing pool almost daily and playing cards with the boys every weekend we were allowed to. I learned more just hanging out with Mr. Esdridge than I can calculate. I never looked upon him as a peer but with the respect he deserved and that's why we stayed friends for so long. I remember when he died, it was a loss for sure. If a young person ever gets a chance to become close to an older person, they should take advantage of such a situation for as long as possible and learn what you will.) At Roy's, they had a model car racing set and I had never seen one before and remember being fascinated by such a thing. We played until Roy got bored then we went outside and met his dog who his brother had trained. I met his older sister Margaret who didn't even turn her head to say hello to such a kid, and I met his little brother Donald. That was about it.

THE FARM

The Esdridges worked a small farm. i was invited one day to go to the farm by Roy. I was excited to go. Outside of St. Louis we went and when we arrived, I was introduced to the smells of a rabbitry. I immediately handed a broom to Jim, Roy's brother, and off we went to sweep the daily load of rabbit crap from about 250 cages, a necessity to keep the place clean and the rabbits healthy.

I didn't mind, because Roy was leader of the pack and if he did it, we did it. After about an hour and a half of shoveling and sweeping and feeding and watering, we started out of the rabbitry when Roy's dad told us to stand back and we watched as Roy's older brother Lenny led a cow, sorry, the cow, up a hill and shot it in the head. Quite gruesome for a city kid to watch. Then Roy's oldest brother Teo (a veterinary doctor) cut the animal's throat. We got up close then and watched the poor creature die. After about an hour, the animal was packed into a truck, and I guess headed for the packing house.

A good education all around for one day. I spent over thirty years at the farm. Days in and days out, weekends, whole summers, in every type of weather. And each day was different. I became part of the crew, getting chewed out when doing something wrong, getting a nod when going the extra mile, but we were never paid. The hard work and self-sacrifice and education was paid I suppose. I guess you could say I came out ahead without sounding too cliché.

FARM SUMMER

Roy and I spent three full summers on the farm, during the Beach Boys hey day and kept the place up, clearing weeds from buildings, taking care of a sick horse, and just general daily work. Oh yeah, and Roy was raising a beehive for the honey.

This one summer was going just about as expected, hot, we only had fans and a hose we stood under when things became intolerable. But we had our music and freedom, a fairly good radio, cigarettes, and about fifty cans of chicken noodle soup. For some reason, Roy's mother only bought chicken noodle soup.

Roy and I both smoked at fifteen years old because we started out as looking peer level "cool" and got hung up on nicotine. We didn't drink except for Kool Aid and at the farm we didn't have a pitcher, so we used a big bowl and dipped a cup into the bowl to get some red sweetness. We didn't have any ice either. Roy kept the bowl by his bed upstairs and also the cigarettes which were rationed by Roy. Well, one day I decided to steal a cigarette, reached for the pack, and accidentally dropped the whole pack into the Kool Aid. I grasped the pack out as fast as I could, but the damage was done… red Winston cigarettes!

I put everything back as was, scooped the tobacco bits out of the bowl, and tore ass down the steps and outside I went. After a while, I noticed Roy head for the house and I stepped for the rabbitry, in case I needed a running start before an ass kicking. Roy went into the house. A few seconds later, he yelled for me to come to the house near his upstairs window. I hesitated, but he said he wasn't going to kick my ass for the cigarettes. I believed him, he never lied. I went towards the window.

Roy threw out my clean clothes and said, "Watch this!" He put a shotgun out the window (a .410 gauge) and shot my clothes which were on the ground. "I guess we're EVEN NOW for the red cigarettes!" Roy yelled.

He was pissed. I got away lucky.

We tried using the oven to dry out the cigarettes, but they tasted terrible. We went on a two-day smoke out. We used to come home every Friday and weekend so I could work my paper truck job. And when we got home, it took us ten minutes to run to the confectionary down the street to get some smokes!

HIGH SCHOOL

Eighth grade was uneventful At St. Mary and Joseph's School, except for Joy Bellaille who Roy Orbison wrote a song about only she never came walking back to me.

I went freshman year to Bishop DuBourg High School because my mother thought that would be best, but it was not a good idea. I later discovered I should have been a Dutchman from the start, at Grover Cleveland High School. Too much religion at DuBourg. Roy went to Bishop DuBourg High, and I met Vance Buffalo and Ed Lybarger, the only redeeming values of my freshman year.

I went to Grover Cleveland High School starting my sophomore year. Great school is an understatement. Great kids is definitely an understatement. Mr. Vogelsang was my homeroom teacher the entire time I went to this great public school and each class was led by a teacher who wanted to be there. My German teacher was so interested in my German history, she made me get up before class to talk about my experiences. German class held a special place also in my life history. That's where I met Karen B, my second girlfriend. She started it anyway with a "Hello" note. I would have been less surprised to receive the Nobel Prize. She was beautiful. And I was a sophomore while she was a junior sending me a note in class... Wow!

Well, Karen and I met after class, and she said she'd like me to come over to her house and meet with her friend and maybe talk and listen to some music together. I choked up an okay and got directions to her home.

Roy helped me travel to Karen's house to meet her and he gave me pointers on what to do and what not to do. Karen used to go to the roller-skating rink almost every day and begged me to go with her, but I couldn't skate. My ankles were by now really deteriorated, although I was good at hiding it (I wore new shoes that were high ankles), and I'd have to turn down Karen's invitations. Well, she got tired of a guy with no car and who wouldn't go skating. I lost. But I did learn the fine art of kissing, or so I thought.

I turned fifteen years old, and my parents pushed me into getting a weekend job that paid. I used to help Roy at the farm but didn't get paid, that was a buddy helping a buddy thing. I had a pushcart two-mile paper cart route that I did every weekend, but I was tired of that job after two years and went looking for another kind of job. I saw a sign on a paper truck that said hiring. I was with Roy, and he stopped, and I went and talked to the old man who ran the paper truck, and he hired me for fate's determination to work off the back of the truck delivering newspapers to houses. We'd work nights and early mornings to deliver to about 500 homes. I'd be paid $15 for thirty hours work all during the weekend. I did this every weekend, never missing a weekend, no matter the weather, for three years until I was run over, and my leg was wrenched from my body in a road wreck.

The money I needed for Pepsi, cigarettes, and a Twinkie or two, and the job kept me thinned out, but it was a dangerous way to make a buck. Dodging cars while running from house to house with an armful of papers, dodging dogs and mean kids who just targeted you for a beating for no good reason at all. But when I turned sixteen, I had to almost give up this career because of the polio braces the doctors made me wear. I couldn't run with the damn things on.

(Side note: I have a neuromuscular dystrophy disease which I inherited from my mother's side. The nerves die out that feed pulses to the peripheral muscles. Your legs and ankles deteriorate to atrophy phase. Your hands go the arthritis way, curling and knotting up. I type with two fingers. The pain goes away with Tylenol or whatever narcotic your doctor will give you. I learned to tolerate the whole bunch of nonsense because I wanted to stay and keep up with "normal". I worked until I was overtaken by the disease. It's especially hard when your fourteen to seventeen years old trying to meet the opposite sex. It seemed every time you're trying to stay cool, you trip and fall. All you can do is look at the floor behind you as if something on the floor tripped you.)

The paper truck job was more important to me than the braces, so the braces went under the bed. And I stayed with the paper truck job.

Sydney, my boss and the truck operator, needed me more than ever by the second year because sometimes he forget what streets we'd have to go down to deliver papers to, and sometimes he forgot which house got a newspaper and which was not a customer, but all in all, we got along and became good partners together and good friends.

THE WRECK

It was like any ordinary Saturday morning in October, kind of cool, cold enough for me to wear my new padded wind breaker, the perfect blue in color. I decided not to wear my braces this night again, too damn aggravating. I was having a cigarette on the front porch waiting for Sidney, who was late, when all of a sudden, he pulls up across the street as usual.

I jump off the porch and run up to catch on to the back of the truck, grip a rail and yell, "Let's go!"

And off we went.

We made an immediate right turn down Haven Street and headed towards Broadway. I surveyed the back of the truck and noticed Sidney had picked up the *Globe* papers we needed, maybe four bundles. I wire clipped the first bundle open while Sidney hit Broadway, and I started to roll and tie off the first set of papers, knowing I'd have to start throwing to houses soon on the right side of Broadway as we headed towards the Patch. Sidney slowed as we came up to the first yards near the firehouse. I was good and could roll a throw right up to the porch via a soft landing on the grass.

We stopped at the Broadway Bus loop café for coffee and Sidney goes in while I light up a cigarette and keep rolling papers in anticipation of hitting the Patch run, which had so many customers living so closely together there would be little rolling and tying time. Sidney comes out with the coffee, and we take about two minutes to finish the hot drink and smoke. Neither of us has said more than hello to each other since I got on the truck. We were of few words, just getting down to the business we knew together now for three years together. Before I knew it, we were rolling up the loop hill towards the Patch, (so named because of all the tar patches in the streets).

The houses were all on the right and that night I was on target like an ace, no stopping to put a missed shot over a fence, and no hits against a storm door, which could make a noise loud enough to wake every dog in the neighborhood.

We went through the Patch quickly, I remember. Good This meant we could make a stop at Hoffmeister Funeral Home on Broadway to warm up if we were ahead of schedule. Soon enough, we leaftthe candy factory and headed to the funeral home. There we stopped and banged on the front door and the watchman knew us and let us in for warmth and coffee, his fee, a free paper.

After maybe fifteen minutes, we would leave the funeral home and spit a few papers off to the right of Broadway, not many, just a few, then back on Broadway by the pipe yards and down to the bar near Broadway and Haven, by the metal works. We'd have to pull off of Broadway and drive in the alley of the back of the bar to toss the paper at the back door so that nobody would steal the thing. Then we'd turn around, make a right turn back onto Broadway, and get into the left lane in order to toss several papers at the apartments across the street from the bar.

It was about 2:00 am, I later found out from the police report, that Red Villa's bar was closing and the guy who hit us was leaving the bar and racing to get to the coast guard station off Broadway.

Broadway looks empty to Sidney. I'm busy rolling papers and getting ready to throw across the street to the apartments, these had to be exact shots and we had to slow down. As I turn sideways to prepare to throw, I see the headlights coming right at me *AND IN SLOW MOTION I TURN TO JUMP INTO THE BACK OF THE TRUCK!*

I don't make it.

I feel A ROLLING MOTION... GOING OVER SOMETHING... EVERYTHING IS BRIGHT WHITE... THE ROLLING IS OVER AND OVER... ALL OF A SUDDEN, I FIND MY FACE IN THE CURB OF THE STREET... NO PAIN...

I can remember this feeling because I have it in my sleep and have had it in my sleep for over fifty years.

I TASTE BLOOD AND KNOW I'M ON THE STREET AND I HEAR LOUD NOISES... THE BLOOD IS POURING MORE SO THAN WHE-NEVER I'VE BLED FROM THE FACE BEFORE... I IMMEDIATELY LOOK AROUND BUT CAN'T REC-OGNIZE ANYTHING BUT MY TENNIS SHOE WITH SOMETHING IN IT ABOUT TEN FEET FROM ME!

I SIT UP... NO PAIN BUT A COMPLETE HOT FEELING... I SEE A CAR ALL TORN UP NOT FAR FROM ME... MY MOUTH FEELS FUNNY AND I CAN ONLY BREATHE BY BLOWING AWAY BLOOD

FROM MY MOUTH... AS I'M SITTING UP A MAN COMES UP TO ME AND I TRY TO STAND BUT IM- MEDIATELY FALL AND LOOK DOWN TO SEE WHY I FELL AND SEE MY LEG IS GONE AND TWO WHITE THINGS ARE STICKING OUT OF MY KNEE. The man tells me to lay down and I do, and then I start telling him I'm going to die... He ties his belt as a tourniquet around what's left of my leg.

By then Jerry Davis has come to help along with several other people and I hear them remark.

"LOOK AT THAT POOR KID!"

"WHAT THE HELL HAPPENED..."

"HE'S DEAD..."

"LOOK AT ALL THE BLOOD..."

"THERE'S HIS LEG..."

"SOMEBODY GET THE COPS!"

I LAY THERE AND PRAYED. I DID NOT WANT TO DIE, but the cops took forever to get to me. You see, five cars had been involved in the carnage and they were scattered all over Broadway and the ambulance couldn't get to me.

I was put into a 1969 ambulance, an empty converted panel truck and watched them put my leg and tennis shoe wrapped in plastic in the truck with me. Off we went to Alexian Hospital.

At the hospital it was bedlam... I remember hearing,

"THIS KID NEEDS TO GO TO AN ACUTE CENTER..."

"WHAT DO WE DO FOR HIM HERE..."

"STOP THE BLEEDING..."

"GET BLOOD..."

I ASKED FOR A PRIEST... HE CAME LOOKED AT ME AND PASSED OUT OF THE ROOM WITHOUT SAYING A WORD AND JUST TOUCHING MY HEAD... THEY STARTED CUTTING MY CLOTHES OFF AND PUSHING THINGS UP MY NOSE... THE GURNEY STARTED ROLLING AND A GREEN DRESSED MASKED MAN SAID I'D BE OKAY AND JUST TO GO TO SLEEP... I PASSED OUT...

I woke up in a hospital bed dressed in white and screaming in pain! The nurses told me to be still. I looked down my right side and saw my leg was gone... but I was alive. My dad was my first visitor. He just told me to allow the people to help me and do the best I could.

Ray came in next and shook my hand, then Gene came in... <y mother never came in... I don't blame her, my hair was shaved off for head wound sewing and my face was all torn up along with the butchering I took. Who would want to see their kid like that?

The ICU nurses were doing the best they could, but PAIN was the word of the entire situation with anything they did...

(Side Note: Today I'm suffering from osteo myelitis, and two doctors have recommended I have an amputation of the left leg. I told them to go FISH because a bilateral amputee is truly not for me. They claim it's for my life. I again told them GOOD-BYE. I explained the pain after an amputation is tremendous. They argued. I told them experience has been my teacher from 1969, and I haven't forgotten a day!)

Dr. Luh and Dr Schopp, the men who saved my life and my surgeons, both came to see me a few days later and explained to me and my father that they had to take all of what was left of my leg but eight inches because the wound was a rip type of wound and muscles were torn out of the knee area and dirt and oil had contaminated much of the remaining flesh. One day a full-length leg, the next eight inches of a flesh-covered bone.

The pain was so great the doctors gave permission for me to have an extra type of pain killer, to this day I don't know what it was, but it made me goofy. I got goofy with visitors, staff, rehab folks, nurses, and even didn't mind getting into a wheelchair.

REHABILITATION

How does one go about rehabilitating after what happened to me, being torn apart on the street at the age of seventeen years? I mean, where do you start trying to get this kid back to normal thinking much or less regaining ambulation or living with pain as a constant? What do you do as a physical or occupational therapist to diminish the anguish of what is eight inches left of a leg, or lessen the tremendous psychological trauma? All wounds, mental as well as physical, will be ever present and permanent. You do nothing. Medications and therapy are only hopeful band-aids.

I wanted to try and get back on my feet and not be an invalid, my greatest fear. With my physical therapist, Brother Albert, I worked every day. I knew to conquer the cripple tag, I would have to gain strength. Dr. Schopp and Brother Albert built me a leg cast with a crutch bottom that would allow me to peg-leg walk upright between parallel bars and allow the swelling in my stump to shrink in anticipation of wearing an artificial leg. The pain of the cast crutch was intolerable at times and sitting every now and then was a must, but I kept it in my head that it was a way to conquer my disability, so I pushed myself to the point of needing revision surgery. Overdoing it.

I was finally allowed to go home and there I was treated like a king. Waited on by sisters, friends of sisters, especially a girl named Sheryl (an angel for sure) who later married Roy, and many friends came to visit. But I needed a third revision surgery, taking more of what was left of my leg, before I could get measured for an artificial leg.

An above knee artificial leg is designed to free your hands and give you back maybe twenty percent of your walking ability. An artificial leg for someone with less than an eight-inch-long stump and a crippled adjacent leg is a balancing act, period. My first prosthetist Michael Carte Sr. told me that and I am ever grateful for his honesty. He was my prosthetist for over thirty-three years. I am now a patient of Michael Carte Junior and have been for over twelve years. Prosthetists are an amputee's best qualified rehabilitation specialist, and these men knew what needed to be done to get me walking and trained me to walk.

But let's not put too small a responsibility on my recovery on my first post artificial leg (if I may use such a term), girlfriend, Patricia H. My memories of her are unshakable and of the utmost fondness. She had a car. And she'd pick me up and we'd go about anywhere we wanted, fast food restaurants, Cleveland High School, Carondelet Park, ten and twenty miles from home just to brave a faraway trip, and anywhere else our gas money would take us. She taught me how to be in the company of a girl who wasn't my sister without anything inappropriate. We stayed together for several months until my friend (?) stole her away from me and married her! Thanks Gene.

I never fully rehabilitated from my walking disabilities and for those who say, "Oh you'll get used to it."

I only ask, "May I put my boot up your butt and see how long it will take you to get used to the boot?"

Each day is different and that's fifty years of different days and never a "my legs feel good today". But onward I'm supposed to go, and so I do, with God's grace and strength.

BACK TO SCHOOL

I was given private tutoring while I was too incapacitated to go to school and didn't mind the tutor but didn't learn much and missed the companionship of the other students. It was my senior year, and I was anxious to get back to Grover Cleveland High School. And finally, one day I was evaluated good enough on my legs to go back to regular school traffic. Great day.

Mr. Ed Vogelsang made a big deal about me being back in homeroom and the principal gave me a note stating I could always leave class five minutes early in order to beat the traffic to my next class. School meant I was back. Not totally, but back.

The kids, numbering about 450 seniors, took up a collection of lunch chips for me and I got a coffee can full of donations from the class, pretty good for a kid who cashed them all in for a couple of hundred dollars in 1970 money. I graduated with the class of 1970 from the Kiel Opera House.

SUMMER WORK AND GETTING READY FOR COLLEGE

My first job after graduating from high school and during the summer before going to the University of Missouri at Columbia (Mizzou), was at a Burger King restaurant on Lemay Ferry Road. I used to take a cab to work and a bus back home. It was a great job. And by now Roy and Sheryl were pretty thick together and he was no longer a compadre of mine. We were still friends, but Sheryl was, of course, his main attention. Which was fine by me, and any other friends Roy and I had together. Roy and Sheryl used to come into the restaurant, and I'd always stack them up with extras, kinda as a joke. They'd order a bag of fries and when nobody else was working the front I'd give them a full carry out sack of fries. For a whopper I'd stack three patties of meat high and cover it with fixin's.

Working at Burger King wasn't easy for me, but I never complained and did everything I was told to do. One day I was told to sweep the entire parking lot, and so three hours later I had it swept clean. The manager called me into his office while I was putting the trash from the lot away in these monstrously heavy trash bags. I told him to give me a minute to put the brooms away and he said, "Okay." He then told me to clean all the tables during the not busy hour. You had to do this by turning the tables upside down to get underneath the sitting benches and table area. This took some time and a look of cleaning buckets and drying towels, but I managed to get every table done within a two-hour period. I kid you not. I remember the work as if it was yesterday. I was wearing out and my shift wasn't over. I asked Tom the manager if I could leave early because my artificial side was skilling me. I had just done the huge parking lot and emptied the trash I swept and picked up, and then I cleaned all the tables and benches in the dining room, and I wanted to leave two hours early because I was worn out.

This is just how it happened: Tom told me I wasn't working out and he let me go. I was fired before the sweat dried from my forehead. When I asked why, he said the district manager didn't like the way I kept coming up short on the cash register. I protested, saying I never came up shorter than anyone else. I told Tom that I gave my friends some freebees but only once in a blue moon, and Mr. Marks said it was okay (he was my direct supervisor). But Tom just told me to leave, and so I did. My first taste of discrimination.

When I got home early, my mother interrogated me why I was fired, and the reason sent her into a rage, and then she went ballistic. She called Tom at Burger King to get the real reason. He again stuck to his district manager's story. She then called everyone she could possibly think of and ended with a call to Senator Tom Eagleton's office. I'm serious, she did. Two days later, Tom from Burger King called me asking me to come back to work for him, but I refused. I was preparing for Mizzou.

MIZZOU

Going to Mizzou was breathtaking. You don't know where to start thinking. I was roomed at Graham Hall. My roommate's name was Steve Turley, nicest guy on earth. And Vance was on my floor, an old high school buddy from Bishop DuBourg. My dad helped me move in, wished me luck, and off he went. That first day I was busy getting to know Steve and then I went to meet up with Vance and we went on our first of maybe a hundred (slight exaggeration) excursions on campus. The student union was our favorite hangout. A beautiful place where you could get a Coke and watch all the people passing by. It seemed there was a never-ending stream of students coming and going.

As freshman, most of our classes were dictated to us by administration, but I did choose anthropology as the only elective I was allowed. Vance did the same. This is one class I enjoyed, everything else was a labor. Vance and I never had anything but this one class together and I think he made it to a total of two sessions; it didn't interest him at all. But he progressed in electrical engineering.

The campus café was another great hang out, especially during hot weather when the girls used the fountain for cooling off and of course they were just wearing T-shirts. This was a time of free spirits and love.

In English class, I got lucky and met a goddess whose name was Mary Anne Carr. I gave it every strategy I could muster for a semester to get her to acknowledge I was a human and alive but to no avail. She was friendly, talkative, smiling, and would slow up to walk with me but nothing more, and at the end of the semester I never saw her again. Here's wishing her an Irish blessing.

I later discovered there was a girl I knew from high school who was going to Mizzou when I was attending who tried to REACH ME. Years later, we met, and she told me she tried several times to call me at the dorm and left word, but I never got the messages. Good thing anyways I was a sub-species next to her, and had I met her at school it would have turned my class work into nothing. A double Irish blessing to you, Maureen H.

After a year of classes, football games, keggers, doing my own laundry, every now and then driving back and forth to St. Louis, (disabled students were allowed to have cars), panty raids, a Linda Ronstadt concert, mediocre cafeteria food, the smell of incense and pot, music good and bad, I left Mizzou for the year. Anticipating coming back for sophomore year.

BACK HOME

After living on my own at university, moving back home was an ass-kick, but again my choices in life were zero to none. I started looking for employment but also registered for a math class at Forest Park Community College. I don't know why I went to Forest Park, but I know now it was divine guidance, (whether you believe in that sort of thing or not, if you lived my life, you definitely would believe in some kind of help existing, but don't ask me for more of an explanation than "divine assistance"). Because no sooner had I registered at Forest Park than I went down the street a block and put in an application to work at the humane society. They were impressed with my education and without caring about my disability gave me a job in the animal hospital. College made for good cage cleaners, I guess.

59

I wore a green smock and worked in the animal hospital which consisted of three wards of sick and injured animals, pre-operative and post-operative, cats and dogs. My main jobs were to make sure the animals had proper food and water, take their medicine no matter how disguised it had to be, and make sure the animals and their cages were clean and dry. There were two ward attendants for about fifty animals and six veterinarians who would come in and need help checking on their patients. Post-operatives had to be watched for breathing and bleeding and pre-operatives had to be handled because they were the biters, you can be sure of that.

After about a year of being a hospital ward nurse I became a night nurse, whose duties included watching over the entire hospital wards by myself without interference from the doctors. Because a night nurse was just that: someone who worked after closing and after everyone but the building cleaning crew went home. I worked Friday, Saturday, and Sunday afternoons and all night those three days... keeping the puppies and kitties fed, watered, medicated, getting bitten every now and then, watching over the building and truck yard, answering phone calls of panicking pet owners, and letting those come in for emergency services with the resident veterinarian when necessary, and dispatching the truck driver on duty when the police called in for help with an animal. Sometimes all at once.

But I loved the job. Hated the hours. Needed to go back to school.

Another of my responsibilities was to open the buildings up in the morning and let folks in after checking who they were. Those I knew I just greeted with, "good morning"; those I didn't, I asked questions. One cute young lady came in and said her name was Patty and she was a volunteer, and she had a volunteer's card. I definitely let her in. Immediately, my mind went into strategy mode, and I started thinking, 'How am I going to meet more with her?' I spotted her in the hospital ward hallway and made a beeline towards her and started a conversation about the ward patients (of all things), telling her all about how I took care of them all at night. She didn't say much and left for another ward. I knew my attempts at conversation were nixed, but later I discovered she was just shy. I started heading out of the hospital and my boss Bob Baxter stopped me and asked me why I was still at the place, my shift was over, and I remember telling him I was busy being shot down.

He looked down the hallway and saw this Miss Patty and said, "Maybe not."

Well, in my mind thinking over this first meeting with this girl, she didn't tell me to get lost. That was a plus on my side. She just didn't say much and walked away from me. As if that had never happened before to me with women. But no, "Get lost", "Drop dead", "I'm married", "I'm a lesbian", "I'm asexual", and so on... none of that.

I made another attempt the next Saturday when I would be letting folks in, to catch up with her and ask her out. I met her again as luck would have it.

All rehearsed, I said, "Hey Patty, can I talk to you later?" She said, "Okay," and smiled.

I waited in Bob's office for twenty minutes or so because I didn't want to rush her and by now everyone including the doctors is teasing me. I asked her if she lived in the south. She said she lived by Chuck-A-Burger, practically a landmark. I told her I did too (although I lived fifteen miles from the place), and we made a date that I would pick her up from the humane society when her volunteer shift was over and take her to Chuck-A-Burger and then home before I had to go back to work. We did just that.

Although my life challenges with my disability continue and are getting more difficult as I get older, that date with Miss Patty at Chuck-A-Burger that day told me I was on my way to being physically rehabilitated!

The Blue NOVA

When I was in my last weeks at Mizzou, my father helped me buy a 1971 Chevrolet Nova, navy blue in color, using part of my $23,000 settlement money, (that's all I got for being butchered on the street, about $23,000). I fell in love with this new car.

I remember driving this thing constantly at the university. Since I was one of a few in Graham Hall who had a car on the floor, I was always being asked for favors and thus I became a popular kid. One day in particular sticks out. I was asked to fetch a keg of beer and pouring sprocket for a kegger the floor was having at the softball field one Saturday afternoon. I went to the liquor store and got the keg, no questions asked since the guy at the store thought only upper classmen had cars on campus. I took the keg to the softball field and noticed everyone had a chick with them but me. The story of my life then. The guys slapped me on the back, took the keg out of the trunk and told me to stay and drink and play ball. But being stag and trying to save face, I said no, I had another party to go to. Well, I then drove off the field as quickly as I could and then for about two hours just drove around campus doing nothing but driving my NOVA. After two hours, I decided to go back to the softball field since these were my friendly floor brothers anyway and noticed as I was driving up to the field, they were all running towards me. I stopped the car and got halfway out, and they gang-tackled me in a friendly way, took my keys, opened the trunk, and took out the pouring sprocket to the keg which I accidently drove off with when I delivered the keg. They had been without beer for about two hours.

But when I became a civilian again, I think having my NOVA helped me capture Miss Patty. She took the bus everywhere, and here I had a relatively nice car. I needed every advantage I could get. And my NOVA with an eight-track player in it was an advantage I needed to secure more than one date with such a shy girl.

Patty and I worked at the humane society in our different occupations. She was hired as a veterinarian assistant and I was still a night nurse on weekends, which put a damper on weekend dating. But like always, we made do… maybe practice for the long-term future.

By now I was also a full-time student at Meramec Community College, I decided not to go back to Mizzou, I had too much going on in my life to leave St. Louis. I didn't regret it or give it a second thought. And at Meramec, I was just taking general transfer studies trying to gather enough credits to go to the University of Missouri at St. Louis. My plan. A history major. Then maybe teaching, yet all still vague.

The NOVA kept running everywhere I had to go and every now and then needed a tune up. Well, who was the best plug and points man in the territory, but my Uncle John. He had the tools and since the NOVA was stripped down (little of anything attached to the engine, no power steering, brakes, or air conditioning), an expert like Uncle John could make it hum. Aunt Norma didn't mind us working on the car except for the beer we over-drank. And she probably had other things around the house for Uncle John to do, but once we got involved in the NOVA, that's all we did. It's called imposing.

The NOVA is responsible for being a cupid and an anti-cupid under a different set of circumstances. I used to roll into Cuba to visit my cousins Aunts and Uncles and this is before Patty and I had become steady friends. My cousin Anthony never let me leave his sight with the NOVA unless he was with me.

One time when my Uncle Harry sent me to the store near the lakefront to get a watermelon, my Uncle Tommy's new girlfriend asked if she could go along just for the ride and of course I said sure.

As we were pulling out, Anthony jumped through the car's back window and said, "Don't forget me!"

I don't know how he fit through the window. but he made it inside while we were moving. So, the three of us went to the market, checked the place out, and laughed and joked at Anthony's natural comedic routines, especially when he did his monkey routine. When we got back to the clubhouse after maybe an hour, everyone started after us wondering where the heck their watermelon was!

Maybe a year later, same clubhouse, same town, same crazy cousin Anthony, same sharply polished NOVA looked like a mirror. I could Turtle Wax that baby... even the wheel covers. Anthony and I are driving to the market again on the gravel road when what do we spot on the left side of the road but two females walking together opposite our direction, we could see how pretty the girls were. I slowed to a stop. Anthony made a grunting noise and jumped in the back seat as if to hide. I leaned against the window jam and looking straight at two of the most beautiful creatures ever created and said, "Hey."

(Side note: Later, Chrissy would tell me she thought my car and I were cool but thought saying "Hey" was hilarious. And she said she was curious why Tony was so obviously hiding in the back seat. I told her she and her

66

friend were so cute we didn't know whether to stop or keep going, because we had been playing in the fields all day and weren't too presentable. Chrissy laughed. She's in Heaven now.

After saying "Hey," I thought to myself, 'These girls are way out of my league.' I mean Chrissy's dark long hair and beautiful face and the other doll looking just as pretty. What business did I have even stopping near them?

And then I said the next thing that came to my mind, "Need a ride?"

What a toad thing to say. They declined politely of course. At this time, Anthony jumps out of the car and heads over to them and introduces himself. I never saw Tony again in all my travels to Cuba for many years. I was invited to the wedding and Chrissy danced with me and remembered me.

After many thousands of miles, the old NOVA was looking her age and running on maybe not all six cylinders. It needed to be replaced, but with what?

NOVA was no longer a manufactured brand by Chevrolet, and I wanted something different. Not wishing to get ahead of my stories here but having to put to rest the story of my NOVA, please indulge me for a few more sentences. I went to a Chrysler dealer in Evansville, Indiana and gazed upon the Dodge Challenger, a sleek beautiful yellow over white sports machine that was priced within my reach with a trade in. Goodbye navy-blue NOVA, with memories that still endure.

MISS PATTY

Patty and I worked together at the humane society for several more months in our different occupations, and after our first meeting at Chuck-A-Burger we went on dates every chance we got. But my job didn't allow many weekend dates because I had to work Fridays through Sundays. But we managed to get together in the evenings and those weekends I called in sick or got off for vacation. We went everywhere we wanted in the NOVA; freedom was our byword. We didn't meet up with any other couples, just stayed within ourselves, going to shows, restaurants, (fast food) is all we could afford.

When I felt it was right, I decided to introduce Patty to my family and over to my parents' home we went. My little sisters thought it funny that Timmy had a girlfriend, my mother asked a million questions, and my dad just said hello and offered a soda. Patty was shy and self-conscious to start with and even after my rehearsals and warnings, she was uncomfortable. So, we didn't stay long for that first meeting and off we sped away in the NOVA, laughing at the predicament we were just in.

Patty desperately wanted to move away from the small apartment she shared with her mother. She was willing to move anywhere when she discovered the apartment next door to my parents' house. It was cost effective, safe, near me and the family, and everything for a single girl. An old man owned the house. He lived downstairs and was harmless. Patty moved in.

Patty had many homemaker skills. She could cook better than most and her spaghetti was deluxe. She could bake. She was clean, and her place was always tidy. She was good with a buck. She could knit and sew and she had a terrific figure, especially a perfect posterior. True. She got compliments on how perfect her butt was from more than just my inebriated friends.

One day after one of my night shifts, I went home only to discover somebody locked the screen door and I had no way to use my key to get into the house. So, my choices were to sleep in the car or go over to Patty's apartment and crash there. Decisions. Patty welcomed me in, helped me get down to my t-shirt and jeans. It was near winter. She didn't mind when I took my damn leg off and asked for a wet cloth to wipe it out and set it next to the bed. She made me a continental breakfast and off to sleep I went. My dad came over and woke me up in time to go home and get ready for my next shift. On walking home, he stopped me and told me never to do that again, staying at Patty's.

He said, "She's got neighbors watching things."

I said to him for butting into my business, "Yes sir," and I never slept at her place again.

VISITING THE MCGUIRKS AND COMPANY

I decided to take Patty to Salem to meet family, Uncle Tony, Uncle Jim, and company and gang. We pulled into town, and I showed her all the places I grew up around and Sacred Heart Church and the convent school building and then we headed to Uncle Jim's to meet the family I was proud of. Things went well, Aunt Mary started cooking something and Uncle Jim showed Patty his garden. We had a good visit and lunch and then pushed on to Uncle Tony's place.

We met Aunt Avella and Uncle Tony with Susan, and had a good visit. We didn't stay too long and then we were off. I remember these first visits because they were visits independent of my folks with Linda, Ronnie, or Larry. We were to make an official visit at the next family reunion get-together at Salem at Grandpa's place when we spent the night. But for now, we just made a cameo visit and back to St. Louis we headed. Get home before dark and don't spend the night anywhere, my father's law.

On the next outing, we went to Cuba to meet up with Uncle Harry and gang, and to meet the friendliest person on earth Rose Brakefield.... a lot of folks showed up and I remember Anthony was missing, but Patty got to see the "A" frame clubhouse, the lake, and she knew fishing more so than I did and I noticed for the first time she turned down a beer for a soda. That's what makes this memory stick in my head. We headed back to St. Louis late, but my dad was strict about no overnighting while just dating, so me and the NOVA were careful with our cargo and a landing on Michigan Avenue we made it about midnight.

On another excursion to Salem, I decided to go hunting with Patty at Grandpa's place with Larry as the official guide. I had just gotten myself a .410 shotgun and decided I'd clear the woods of the two squirrels that lived on Grandpa's forty acres. Well, Grandpa didn't care and off we went attracting cockleburs, ticks, and chiggers. After an hour of walking the woods, I started firing into the trees and Larry did the same with his .22 rifle. We never tried to hunt the rabbit that lived at Grandpa's place.

We got back to Grandpa's house and surveyed the damage to our jeans and boots, legs and ankles, and then agreed hunting for those two squirrels should be left to the hardier fellows.

The entire McGuirk family contained good fellows, and no one was really a misfit, and the women were exemplary. I never had to warn Patty about meeting any of my relatives and to grow up with these people was truly a blessing, but why? Because they were just good, moral, conscientious hard-working folks who understood the value of raising good kids. The men had one weakness and that was too much drinking at times, and some short tempers but everyone can attest to repentances. My dad's temper usually didn't last before he'd regret what he had done, and he left a good life to follow: stick with it.

MEETING PATTY'S FAMILY

Patty's grandmother Gi Gi was a joy to meet and know and Patty loved her very much. Her grandfather Foley on the other hand gave me the cold shoulder for thirty years and he and I kept our distance. Me out of respect for him

73

and I think he didn't care too much for me but accepted me for Patty's sake. I've been trying to figure out how to start this section of my memoir, which has to be told. If I include someone like Patty, my most important soulmate meeting my family, it's only right I tell the story of me meeting her family.

Patty's Aunt Nancy was fun for a story or two, but she was also very religious, and I wasn't, but I enjoyed talking to her. Patty's Uncle Bud was a great guy, a jokester, and a ball of fun when backs were turned.

On the Alles family, I only knew grandmother and grandfather and they were welcoming but that was about it, just too elderly to have much to do with us kids.

Patty's Aunt Bert was a nice lady and Uncle Carl was a great guy.

Patty's cousins have dispersed across the country and sadly they don't communicate, but I understand they are good people, along with her cousin Laura.

ONWARD AND UPWARD

My mother decided to go to Canada one fall day, and she explained if Lloyd and I drove the NOVA with Janet, Carolyn, and her in the backseat. we could make the trip easily. So, we did. Chevrolet outdid themselves when they built the NOVA six-cylinder for this little car took us to Windsor, Ontario, Canada, and back without breathing hard. In Windsor, we visited with my Aunt Irene and Uncle Roy, and my cousin, Teddy.

We went to Essex, Canada, and visited my grandmother who spoke French better than English. And then Lloyd and I went looking for beer bars and anywhere being an American might get you a free pass. Instead, we got mooned on the roadway.

Lloyd and I did have to babysit Carolyn one day who was about ten years old at the time. She wouldn't quit nagging us, so we put her outside the car and took off for about 300 feet. She ran after us screaming. We let her back in and she was set straight. She still to this day tells this story.

Lloyd and I drove back to St. Louis after a week in Canada, and Patty and I had for the first time in our relationship been apart. I asked her to marry me the next week and we were engaged when she said yes. She didn't hesitate, poor girl. The Canada trip had proven to be gainful for me and the gift I brought back for Patty she still has in her room to this day, forty-five years later. I saw Lloyd maybe thirty years ago, but besides hello, we didn't talk, and I haven't seen him since. It's sad how someone in your history can disappear but that's life, I guess.

MARRIED

After being engaged in early fall of 1972, Patty wasted no time setting us up with a wedding date for May 1973. I remember agreeing to everything, which was the best thing I could have done. Patty was all excited about the upcoming nuptials and I didn't quite realize what I was getting into with the Mass and reception party coming up.

I do remember my left leg was giving me all kinds of problems with weakness overcoming me at work. I tried to wear one of my old braces but that didn't make things any better. For some reason this damn muscular dystrophy had to start acting up at a time like this. I just got tough and dealt with it.

My mother and sisters came to Patty's aid when her own mother and relatives decided they didn't want to get involved with the wedding preparations, except for Grandmother Gi Gi who held a surprise wedding shower I gave away. I asked Patty maybe a week before the shower if her mother would be going to her wedding shower at Grandmother Gi Gi's house? Patty still laughs at that brainer.

I was getting all kinds of advice about this time from different friends and relatives, but two that I'll never forget came first from Roy, who said to me in a serious tone and manner, "You're lucky."

And the second thing told to me came from my father who said, "Make it work."

To which I retorted with a "Yes sir."

I remember getting fitted for the tuxedos with Uncle John, my best man, and Vance, a groomsman. I remember that's when it hit home what I was doing and getting into. Unfortunately, I had to go to the limb shop after being fitted while the other boys partied because my artificial leg was breaking down while my left leg was just uncontrollable. I was in trouble. Nothing like I had gone through before.

At the limb shop, they had to repair the knee (several hours of work) and then they told me maybe nerves were bothering me on my left side since I did have the neuromuscular disease and told me if I couldn't wear my brace then I should wrap my entire leg with elastic bandages and stay off it until I could see a doctor. I had too much to do to let this damn set of legs lay me up.

It's now the wedding day and while we men were waiting in the church vestibule, Patty's Uncle gave us some airline bottles of booze and told us, "These are what you need right now," and he left as quick as he came. Vance inhaled two bottles, mine was vodka and down it went. Uncle John wasted no time with his bottle. Then the priest called us to the front of the interior of the church.

I've never been so afraid in my life and that's no exaggeration, everyone looking at us and we having to walk to the center of the aisle. I told my artificial leg if it failed me, I'd have a public burning of the damn thing! My left leg I just concentrated on.

When I saw the bride, my mind turned blank, and I just took her in... no thoughts or thinking... just blank ogling... just blank ogling...

Writing here is tough because all I remember was the bride... I knew a priest was there saying something and telling me to say something and I know I was in a church, but after that, I was next to a bride... On command from the priest, I remember turning around holding the bride and walking out of the church and then meeting people I don't remember at the back of the church while standing next to the bride, who everyone was kissing.

I came to in the car me and the bride were sitting in when the driver started honking the horn.

The reception was a blast and everyone I knew was there partying hardy... all friends and relatives... dancing... libations flowing... laughing! I danced with everyone and the legs held up under sheer fortitude... fun, we did have... fun!

Patty and I finally were allowed to call it a night and home we went... both too tired to do anything, I remember, but to open the wedding envelopes and count the loot... And off to sleep we went!

We went to Branson for our honeymoon for five days and did what tourists do in Branson, had a good time but had to take it easy because of my leg problems and back home we came with Patty driving most of the way back home.

It was good to get back home and see close family again with all the festivities over.

BACK TO WORK

I was at J. E. Hanger and Company, and the first thing I did when I got back to my work bench was to find people had just piled work on my desk with no explanation or name tag of who it was from or what it was for. Very frustrating, but I was low man on the totem pole and so I had to sort things out the best I could.

While I was working that first day back, I was called downstairs and told, I remember this distinctly, by Mr. Gar Mart that the crew was going on strike and since I was too new to join the union, yet I would be expected to continue working, unless the union thought differently. Great. Over the next two weeks I spent time learning how to write a resume and sent it out to every limb shop in town. I wanted nothing to do with a union fight against a bunch of guys I just started working with.

Well, no sooner had I been ready to leave J. E. Hanger's than Mr. Hanger calls me into his office and offers me a job as an apprentice prosthetist in Evansville, Indiana. Working directly with a certified prosthetist in a two-man shop with the promise of going to school to learn prosthetics at Northwestern University in Chicago. I fell over myself saying yes, I'd go, with no idea where the heck Evansville, Indiana was. On a map, Mr. Hanger showed me.

I was really excited to tell Patty the exciting news when I got home, and I blurted out how much of an opportunity this would be for our future.

She said, "Where's Evansville, Indiana?" and then looked at me as if I had three heads! I explained everything and kept waiting for a pleasing look to come over her face but all I remember seeing was question marks. Maybe it's how I was telling it?

I talked to Mr. Mart at Hanger's the next day to call Patty and explain it, and he did. This time when I got home, she had the look of being scared and told me if it was something I wanted to do, she was all for it.

(Side note: It was an arduous move and stay at Evansville for Patty right from the beginning. Being away from everyone she knew and her entire family, she would not have lasted a month with me either considering the difficulties we went through if it had not been for getting to know and work for one man, Cecil Johnston.

EVANSVILLE, INDIANA

We had a mobile home we were buying since apartment living had been a big turn off for both of us and we couldn't afford a built home yet. So we had purchased a mobile home and with the property rent in Fenton, Missouri, it was reasonable to afford. So, when we decided to move to Evansville, Indiana, it meant moving our home with us.

We took a trip to Evansville for one week with the intent to look at the town, find a place for our mobile home, and meet the people I was going to work with. We found some nice ground in a historic town named Newburgh, Indiana. Next, we went into town and met the folks at J. E. Hanger, Company of Evansville, both of them. Cecil Johnston and Mrs. Betty Sanders, both of whom were really friendly and welcoming. We all had no idea how big an impression Mrs. Sanders or Cecil would have on our young lives. Memories of them are impressed in my mind and it is difficult to write about them as in the long ago past.

The shop was tiny, with two patient rooms, a waiting room, and the shop area split in half, machine shop in one area and supplies on the other side. Cecil had several limbs in fabrication status and showed me some of his work. Later, I discovered Cecil was so good a prosthetist that he did prosthetic work during surgery at the local hospitals. He was that trusted by the doctors in the area.

Without saying a word to him, Cecil told me his first project with me was to make me a new limb I could walk with, it was that obvious that I was having so much trouble with the damn thing I was trying to wear.

Patty and I left Evansville more confident that it was a good prospect for a future, and we got home and started packing and notified Morgan Moving Company that we would need our home moved to Newburgh, Indiana. They agreed, and a contract was signed. I should have kept the pen the contract was signed with because that's all Morton Moving Company's efforts and goodwill would have been worth.

The move was timed to have taken nine hours. It took three days, and our mobile home was torn to pieces. The home should have been emptied of furniture to make it light enough to travel, but Morton Moving decided they could get the job done quicker and easier without unpacking the home and the tires blew off the wheels and ripped the rear of the home apart about halfway to Newburgh.

I had to chase down a repair crew and a tire company, I must have driven 250 miles during that period. Finally, it was patched up good enough to travel. We made it to Newburgh, Indiana. The man who owned the property where we were going to park our home saw the damage and told me to get insurance information from Morton. When I asked the driver for his insurance information, he told me it was not their fault the tires blew and if I wanted them to detach the mobile home, I had better pay them their money in cash!

I had no choice. My insurance company, MFA, claimed it was not their responsibility since the mobile home was in transit. I had to spend what savings Patty and I had to get our home repaired. It was fixed as good as new.

Patty and I slowly but surely met our neighbors. We were shy, and we first met Bud and Nellie Wentzel. Bud was a siding salesman when aluminum siding was big, and Nellie was just Nellie. We lived across the road from Bud and Nellie and Bud always invited us over for barbeque and he always had the coldest beer.

We tried to return the favors with our neighbors, the David Days were a fine family, and Dave and I could sometimes be found at Frenchie's Bar on occasion.. In fact, that's where the two of us watched Nixon resign. But we never stayed late, we were working stiffs with wives who didn't drink beer.

Storms in Indiana were notorious and severe in the area we lived in; Vanderburgh and Jasper Counties. Patty became a storm watcher with Bud while I just worried that mobile homes always got the worst of it when storms hit. Luckily, we never ran into any damaging weather while in Indiana.

I started my work at Hanger's with Cecil as soon as things settled down with our mobile home. Being in a small shop, Cecil started me off doing an inventory so I could familiarize myself with all the materials we kept within the building. I learned quickly that we had to keep up with ordering repair parts because there were so many parts needed and we could not keep everything in inventory. I also had to become an expert at prosthetic sock sizes and fits, and there seemed to be a different fit for every different patient.

Before long, Cecil had me assist him with fabrication of limbs, something I had never done at the main shop in St. Louis, and one of the first legs I poured resin on was the new shin to the new limb Cecil was slowly but surely building me. Since it was a freebee, we had to do it in our spare time, but we used new parts.

Cecil and I worked together for forty to forty-five hours per week, he showed me how to wait on patients, do minor repairs, saving the big stuff for him or we would send major breakdowns to St. Louis for repair. It got to a point where Cecil could take a day off and leave the shop up to me for a day or two, and those times Cecil was called away to hospitals to see patients, it was easier for him knowing I could handle things at the shop with Mrs. Sanders or by myself. This independence earned me a recommendation to St. Louis that I be sent to Northwestern University in Chicago for studies in prosthetic science. Mr. Hanger agreed. But first things first.

Patty notified me she was with child. I didn't know what to think! My mind went blank again in excitement!

I thought out loud, "The loser might now start becoming a winner!"

That thought rolled around in my head the whole time I was in Northwestern University, and while Patty was pregnant.

Cecil was happy for me, and we scheduled the Northwestern trip right away, which is not what we really wanted to do. Cecil wanted to go over some studies for a few weeks before I went to school so I'd be more prepared, but now timing was everything. I'd have to go "green".

(Side note: In my entire educational career, I've always gone "green". As an army brat, I went to ten schools in eight grammar grades, two high schools as a teenager, and in college I went first to Meramec Community College, then University of Missouri for general studies, Northwestern University for prosthetic science, University of Evansville for data processing, back to Meramec Community College for math, Maryville University graduating in business machine management, Webster University for an MBA, and Webster University for a masters in information science... Always "green" with little work experience except in prosthetics.)

Before I could leave for Chicago, I had to have one of my infamous sebaceous gland infections taken care of at the local hospital. This was acutely painful and laid me up for a day I didn't have time for. I was prone to get sebaceous gland cysts the entire forty-five years I wore an artificial limb. They would swell up under the skin with fluid, then become infected, then have to be surgically removed. I would have one removed about every three months or so; it became a routine for me. And it was just a part of my wearing a limb. Several times I had to have two removed at the same time and they were painful coming and going.

But finally, we left for St. Louis, Miss Pregnant and me, and I left on a plane for O'Hara. Chicago was a high, but it soon dawned on me that I didn't know a soul in this entire city. I was roomed at the Allerton Hotel because the guest dormitories at the university were full.

School was cool. I took on many friends, other misfits from out of town, the Allerton bar was a player's spot, I kept my nose clean... the food was always gourmet, the rooms were beyond nice, on calls home, I'd tease everyone about the luxury.

I picked up quite a bit in class but missed a lot that was over my head, my volunteer patient gave me a "B" grade at the end of the semester, and back to St. Louis I went. And from there to a small prosthetic shop in Evansville, Indiana.

BACK TO ST. LOUIS

Once back at the shop from Chicago, Cecil and I talked laughingly about the Allerton Hotel and the goings-on there with the student body when class was over for the day.

At Northwestern University, I did learn quite a bit concerning the measuring and fitting and fabricating the below knee prosthesis. I had to demonstrate to Cecil I knew what I was talking about and the next new patient's limb for below the knee who came in was all mine. I did well during the entire four-week process from measurement to fabrication with little supervision and Cecil was impressed but not confident I could handle the job entirely by myself, still too inexperienced, practical wise.

I mainly tended to my old duties at the shop, of keeping up with material needs, waiting on patients with needs

I could handle, repairs, and resin fabrication. Cecil told me we should prepare for my next venture to Northwestern University which would be coming up in the Spring. It was December and Patty was big with a baby.

It was Christmas time and Patty and I invited Bud and Nellie and a few other neighbors over to the house for some wine and cheese. About halfway through the festivities, Patty's water broke, and it was off to the races to St. Mary's Hospital in Evansville from Newburgh where we lived. I DROVE STEADY AND SHE WAS CALM, BUT WE WERE IN A HURRY. Getting to the hospital with not too much time to spare. Mary Anne was born on Christmas Eve 1974 in Evansville Indiana. A nurse came out and told me the news and told me that mom and baby were doing fine. There goes the mind again... blank happiness!

After a couple of hours of just sitting in the waiting room and every now and then getting to visit Patty, but not Mary, I headed home completely worn out and beyond hungry. Absolutely no place was open after midnight except for a Quickie gas station. I went in and grabbed a bag of chips and a can of beef stew (spare the brand name but I remember it). To a lighted house I pulled up, Nellie and Bud left the lights on for just such an occasion. I ate half the can of stew, and the dog refused the rest. Two beers later and I fell asleep on the couch. I woke up at daylight and called home in St. Louis. All I could hear once I asked for mom was screaming of my little sisters in excitement over the upcoming news. Mom was pretty happy, and I announced it was a girl and everybody was okay. Then I prepared a trip back to the hospital.

When I saw Patty again, she was crying and in a fit because I was missing. I told her what I had been up to, and she just got even more upset, good for me. I saw Mary for the first time on Christmas Day. I made more happy welcoming phone calls and one to Cecil on Christmas Day. He was happy and I remember he said to me, "I can't imagine you being a dad." Thanks boss…

Soon Patty and Mary got home, and things finally settled down a little and I went back to work, only too happy to be at the shop again. Over the next few weeks, family from St. Louis came and went to see the baby and we made the trip to St. Louis ourselves several times. During this time, Cecil was preparing me to go back to Northwestern.

Patty and I sold our mobile home in Newburgh and moved to Evansville proper. We moved into a nice home but an older home that needed some paint on the inside and other minor work. Mary was baptized in Newburgh with Bud and Nellie standing in as her godparents.

As time flew by, I decided to get enrolled at the University of Evansville, which we now lived two blocks from, and decided I'd take some courses in this new set of studies called data processing. It sounded interesting and before I knew it, I was enthusiastic about what was going on with these machines that read punched cards, typed words, and gave directives on monitor screens, and punched out more cards and paper printouts. The machines we played and worked with in 1974 and 1975 were small room size and made quite a bit of noise, but the amazing thing was they were fast. The University of Evansville was pure enjoyment at night and on weekends. It made me forget about cold beer time and I walked to school and back without a complaint.

Cecil thought any type of education was worth the effort and okayed my going to the University of Evansville and Mr. Hanger agreed and paid for it. But one day after work, I came home to a crying Patty and Mary Anne and Patty blurted out, she missed her family and wanted to return to St. Louis. She claimed she had no one in Evansville, no friends or family. Bud and Nellie had just moved to Ft. Wayne and that, "I was always gone somewhere." I felt sorry for her and couldn't argue with her and so I decided to talk things over with my folks and Cecil first thing.

Patty won the situation.Cecil told me, "You won't work out here if your wife is miserable at home." And my mom and dad agreed. We were moving back to St. Louis. I gave up more than a lot to make for a family, and the future looked a little less dynamic, but it was like my dad had told me, "Make it work."

BACK TO ST. LOUIS

Once back in St. Louis, my career nightmares began. Patty wanted to get an apartment near my family in south county and that was where we planted ourselves while I went back to work at J. E. Hanger in downtown St. Louis, thirty miles one way. Hanger's in St. Louis was a union shop and I was considered an apprentice, whether partly educated or not, and every apprentice had to work for a journeyman or consider himself a near-custodian, cleaning up the resin and fabricating messes.

This was really where I found myself, cleaning bins of leather and trimming resin pours, nasty work beneath someone who just a few weeks ago, was preparing for his second semester at Northwestern. But Mr. Hanger had little control over the union and the members knew it.

I started putting out word to other shops I had a resume and was hoping for a chance to get the hell out of

Carl Belch's dungeon. He was the closest thing to a journeyman they connected me to, and he never spoke a word to me that I can remember.

I heard from Mike Carte who asked me to come in for an interview. I did okay, I guess, in the interview. But later was told I oversold myself to a pair of men who had been looking for someone who could take over both their responsibilities. I stayed for six weeks before I had to quit. Things were so bad for me that I quit knowing I would not qualify for unemployment benefits. I quit with a family to feed too.

My family was at stake, and I just could not find a job in prosthetics or data processing without more education or experience. I went to place after place and knew I was getting shot down because of my disabilities without question. I finally landed at a private employment agency who sent me to G. C. Services in West Port, forty miles from home one way. I met and interviewed with Mr. Mel Roniker, I hope the 'ole Irish Blessing truly happens to this man, he gave me a job on a ninety-day probation... I stayed two years.

While at G. C. Services, I had to have an infected pilonidal cyst surgically removed. This took a hospital stay at Alexian Brothers' hospital for a week and many a friend from the office came to visit, which made healing a lot easier.

At G. C. Services, I was a collector for Bell Telephone and learned quite a bit about life, and people. Some of the folks who influenced my life positively from G. C. Services, I have not forgotten. I only had to leave G. C. Services because a job opportunity came up at Mercantile Bank that I couldn't turn down.

WORK AND MORE BAD HEALTH

MERCANTILE BANK

At Mercantile Bank, I worked for Mr. Bob Bean, an intelligent and thoughtful man who cared about people and let them know it. I worked in the Mercantile Tower in downtown St. Louis, probably the most beautiful office area and building in the entire area.

My life went through so many changes during my tenure here, only five and a half years, that my memory will now go into overdrive. It also hurts very much to write about this time because my life went well except, I finally lost control of my left leg. No big deal compared to the good time I had working at Mercantile Bank and with the people of my office, plus the bonus of working downtown.

I got tougher because I wasn't giving up this job and that meant at one stretch of time taking the bus to work for three years while Patty took our only car to nursing school. The bus ride was fifty-five minutes each way the express bus way, rain, shine, snow, slush, mud, slow moving old people, etc.

I started in the credit card department trying to roundup lost money and get people to turn in their defunct credit cards. Collecting money and credit cards was something I had done at G. C. Services, and I was good at it, so I immediately reached my quota system at Mercantile. This gained me notoriety among my fellow workers who were used to taking it rather slowly during the month's quota tallies.

Mr. Bean knew what would happen with my quick results compared to the others getting quota later during the month. The accepted knowledge among veteran bank collectors was knowing that getting your quota dollars collected early only got you more work and a greater quota to reach the next month, not bigger rewards. But I was on staff for only three months and wanted to make an impression. Mr. Bean then divided the office into those who scored early and those who did not. This seemed to keep the peace among the employees and made for less internal friction.

You had to look sharp while at Mercantile, a suit or at least a blazer and nice shirt and always a tie was required. I remember sometimes it was competitive among some of the people to try and out dress one another, which was fun to watch. The ladies were always fun to watch, and I mean there were some dolls working within an arm's reach of you and you had to keep up professional regard. Damn tough job sometimes.

Jack Kelly and I worked together for many years and became friends. Jack was better than anyone else when it came to collecting delinquent credit cards, his only peer was a man I used to go fishing with, Norm Athee, both men were true assets to the bank. I had a friendship with Terry Coffman who used to laugh at me whenever I stumbled with these damn legs. He didn't do it out of meanness, he just couldn't help himself. I have good thoughts of Terry.

And then there were the hospitalization times. I had another infected pilonidal cyst removed which cost me four days of work. I hated missing work because of illness or ailments, but I was cursed to endure the dreaded complicated dimensions of diseases. I had two infected sebaceous gland cysts removed at once in the operating room while awake because of the danger of full anesthesia during bleeding.

I insisted on going back to work, but my doctor told me not to wear my artificial leg. So, I went back on crutches with my right pant leg pinned up. It beat staying at home with nothing to do. Well, I got more looks and questions than a few from people I worked with at the bank who knew I had a bad leg because of my limp but didn't know I had an amputation. It got so bad that my buddies who would be with me on our travels to the lunchroom or breakroom, would tell people it was an 'old football' injury, or a car wreck 'last week'. Or all sorts of hilarious nonsense, and half of it was believed by some folks.

Going back meant I needed help getting and fetching printouts and papers and notes from others by the secretarial staff. When I went back, beautiful little Judy, who I nicknamed "Pooh" as in Pooh Bear, helped me with everything. She was another brain and arm to everyone. Without her, we would not have done half of what we did accomplish. I worked with Judy the entire time I was at Mercantile. Lucky me.

We collectors and credit card collectors had support staff of all types who we depended on very much for their skills, Gloria was a true asset to anything I ever accomplished and then we had a skip tracer named Linda. She could find anyone, and my file contained by now, I had been there about five years, the most notorious of credit abusers who were considered "skips". Linda and I worked closely together. We became friends and then became close friends, for respect to her, I'll leave it at that. But as long as I know she's okay, I'm okay.

(Side note: I suppose the memoir should be an avenue for nothing but the truth, therefore those reading for this chapter are reading for just that reason. Please bear with me as I tell the truth without hurting anyone. I stumbled here just like any man would, not like a fool but also like a human being).

My wife has meant the world to me, always has and always will. Oh, there have been hard times in forty-four years. I'm not so naïve as to believe you would not think we've had our problems. But we always survived the tough times and worked things out and learned to live with the scars. I always thought marriage was to pledge with someone you love, but experience has taught me that marriage is for bonding with someone you're devoted to.

MY ALCOHOLISM

My hell in alcoholism started around this period in my life. Everyone I knew was a drinker and a drink at lunch did a soul good. But I overdid it and went tail spinning into bottles of beer and hard booze for eight years. I bought mini bottles of hard stuff and put them in my coat so I'd have something to drink at break time at work. My main concern was where my next drink was coming from. This was not like the good times of drinking beer with my uncles at barbeques or get-togethers, this was alcoholism... drug addiction. This was a demon I had no control over. Until I went to the funeral visitation of my friend Norbert G.

I went there to pay my last respects, but I was functionally drunk. I met his daughter at the door, but knowing I probably smelled like scotch whiskey, I did not hug her. I was drunk, but functional enough to know that she would be upset if she smelled the booze on me, which she probably did anyway. It upset her to the point of no return. Her husband disavowed knowing me. It was Roy and Sheryl.

When I got back in my car to go home, I told myself, "Tim, that's enough!" I secretly tried to join A.A. but was afraid of the stigma. I read about alcoholism and still drank, but I slowed down. I tried to cry over what I had done to my life, my family, and my friends, but nothing came out. I got on the wagon and quit COLD TURKEY by myself with God's help. The toughest thing a drunk can do, but one a drunk can do. Over the next eighteen months, I fell off the wagon about three times, but I knew how to dry out and I did every time. Today, I have been completely dry for over twenty-six years and have not slipped even once.

The Big Change

I enjoyed every day I worked at Mercantile and was getting stock options as bonus pay, but I could not get promoted above a 'Grade 9' collector which was very frustrating. I was stuck at my salary level and got a cost of living raise every year but without an education such as an associate degree or bachelors degree, I could go no further up the proverbial ladder.

My brother-in-law Tim, called me at about this time from Centerre Bank's credit card department and told me they had an opening that was a perfect fit for a senior collector like me. He dressed the sales pitch up so well, that to this day I hate him for what he did. He told me I would easily be promoted to a senior assistant supervisory position. My income would be enhanced accordingly. I would answer to the collection manager only. Tim told me everyone else in the office is barely above novice level. I could not help moving over to Centerre, more money, great sales pitch on the job... Away I went.

I will never forgive myself for leaving Mercantile and moving to Centerre Bank. Tim only sold me on the job because he was leaving Centerre and he would get $100 to find his replacement, which he must have laughingly at the time chose to be me. He cared nothing for me or my future, and family. He knew it was a hellhole to work in.

Leaving Centerre Bank after nine months was the happiest I've been since I could remember. On my exit interview with Centerre, I explained the only reason I was not filing a discrimination suit against Rober (I won't use his name because it will give this monster an advantage over me, and I have a vendetta against him to this day, and that's since 1985) and his boss man, Tote (a weak man who at the time thought I was a joke, but he was just a coward)! The only reason I wasn't filing a discrimination suit was because I never wanted to have anything to do with these jerks again! Not even in a discrimination lawsuit!

I hope God forgives me for my anger, but what these three did to me must be punishable. I won't describe what Rober did to me because this memoir is written mainly for my grandchildren. But remember, evil, vile men wear masks that can be seen through if you look close enough because their despicable mannerisms and ways of dealing with others sometimes accidently shows itself. Beware of "nice" guys who want something of you.

CREDIT UNIONS

I got a job at Telephone Credit Union on Hampton Avenue only about ten miles from home. This was a small credit union made up of fifty-two employees three of which, including myself were men. But this place was busy, serving all the telephone workers in the area and having only three offices. I worked at the main office with Mr. Bill Runn, another man I hope the Irish blessing comes true for.

The credit union hired me as collection supervisor because of my experiences and because they were 'bleeding' bad loans. It was almost unbelievable for someone like me to see the amounts of money given out in t-he past of the credit union on such flimsy credit authority. Mr. Runn was hired by the government insurance agency to try and save the credit union from going 'under water' because of the bad loans. I did what I could right from the start but at the time and I told Mr. Runn this after three months' work, the job of recovering a lot of the delinquent loan money was going to be next to impossible. I repossessed more cars that first few months than we had places to put them. We had to charge-off and write-off hundreds of thousands of dollars of bad loans while trying to stay viable.

Mr. Runn and I made the post-dispatch sunday business section one weekend for trying to save the credit union and I was proud of that along with my fellow employees.

My favorite employees were many, and they helped me get over my sister Janet's death, but I just started drinking more. I was drunk at her funeral and it showed. Drunks can't control their emotions and I lost mine when it was time to say goodbye to my sister in the coffin.

I left Telephone Credit Union when Charles W. took over mainly because I didn't trust him for my future, and he didn't care too much for my writing off so many loan dollars. The CUNA insurance agency was tired of writing off loan dollars at Telephone and merged it anyway, so I didn't leave much except for JoAnn, Sherry, Judy, Cathy upstairs, and Mrs. Lemon.

ANOTHER MISTAKE

I went to work for Art Lieber and Dave. Dave was a drunk and a smooth talker and did another sales job on me, but I had worked with him before and knew not to listen to him. But Art promised me a $2,500 bonus if I'd

LIFE IS SHORT AND AN ADVENTURE

come to work for him and start a collection agency hiring anyone I wanted. I took the offer, but the money was slow coming.

I told Art the first thing we needed were clients. He agreed. I explained to get clients we need a salesperson who knew collections, he agreed. Over the next two weeks we looked for someone to fit the salesperson role when I was given a name, Marie. I knew her vaguely. I called her and asked her to come to the office and interview for the job. She was perfect. Beautiful enough to get any potential client's attention, and smart enough to know it and know the business. Art was smitten. He hired her before the door closed behind her when she left the interview.

Art took Marie aside to show her the ropes, but he didn't trust her with clients and never used her for what she was hired for, to do interface and serve clients. Marie ended up a collector in the office and Art continued failing with the clients new and old.

I again told Art we needed better client material to make any money. He claimed we were not doing the best with what we had and fired me. Kiss nine months goodbye. Art sent the company bankrupt and shortly after committed suicide. Marie got married and lives on a farm. Dave the drunk disappeared. I mean disappeared.

What's Next?

I became a freelance subcontractor working collection accounts for whoever needed help in small business outfits. I landed at Progressive Credit Union. I hoped to get hired here on a permanent basis, but it didn't happen. Part of the reason I missed out on being hired at Progressive was health issues. I had an acute pancreatitis attack while working part time at the credit union.

I remember waking up one night in a lot of pain in my chest, Patty was at work and Mary was only a little kid. I told Mary to call Mom and Patty told her to call someone who could take me to St. Anthony's Hospital. I went to the hospital and after examination and nothing for the pain, which by now was extreme, I was sent home by a doctor who told me his diagnosis was I had acute alcoholic indigestion, and it would go away with some Pepto-Bismol.

In the morning, the pain was now beyond toleration and Patty took me to Alexian Brothers Hospital and the doctors there diagnosed correctly that my pancreas had shut down and slowly but surely all my adjoining guts were shutting down. The pain made me scream out, but they couldn't give me anything for pain until a specialist internist examined me to make sure pain medicine could be administered or immediate surgery was required, I was told to bear with it until the doctor got there.

The doctor got to me after an hour. Yes, a long time I remember. He gave me some morphine and put me out! I was in the hospital for eight days before my old pancreas came back to life with just treatment, no surgery, and this meant no food or water for eight days. I experienced thirst that cannot be written about and properly described. It got to the point where I asked for my face to be washed just so I could drink the drips from the washrag, no matter where it had been. Jell-O, I ate without utensils. I just swallowed it out of the bowl. My first foods were rice soup and 7-Up soda… gourmet style!

I missed so much work at Progressive they learned to do without me and after working for a bit there before becoming unemployed for the umpteenth time…

NEXT

Then after being unemployed for a few months from Progressive Credit Union, I went into the hospital for emergency gallbladder surgery, my gall bladder just exploded and took some time for the surgeon to remove and clean it up. I received seventeen stitches and staples plus a hose in my gut to clean up afterward. The doctor wondered what it felt like when I had the attack. I told him it was like a sharp sudden stomachache; he told me it's a wonder I didn't die. No kidding.

When I healed up, a man I worked with slightly before on a job, Dean Reeder came to me and asked me if I'd like to collect for him at Liberty Credit Union for a six-month period. The credit union was in bad shape because of bad loans (how odd for a volunteer run business) and I would help him make some sense of what the credit union had going on and then take leave, just a temporary position. I said yes. But now I went to school at night and some weekends. Taking whatever needed to be taken to use for transfer to a four-year program.

Things at this credit union were in shambles and blame should have landed on the directors and watchdogs from the state inspector's office, but instead, like the dishonest cowards they were, they scapegoated this to the employees past and present and shut the credit union down. I worked here for nine months. My tenure with credit unions and the last credit union I was to ever have anything to do with as an employee.

I now had Patty working full-time and I applied for disability because my disabilities just overtook me.

Continuing Health Complications

I would have enjoyed nothing more than to have gone forward with my education towards a terminal degree or an employment position using the education I had through Maryville University after I graduated and started Webster University in 2000 had it not been for more health problems.

Viral Encephalitis is Fatal

I had an ear infection which led to viral encephalitis, a killer that pierced my blood-brain shield membrane and the infection started to enter my brain.

I had a tonic colonic seizure while at home and luckily Patty was there and noticed the symptoms of a grand seizure and called medical help immediately. The ambulance got there immediately and the EMT was talking to me the whole time. Later I discovered it was to keep me from passing out; it didn't work. I remember the EMT talking, but it was mainly noise. I couldn't make out many words, and I heard a humming sound. I could not see but I knew my eyes were open. Patty said she and Patrick were crying and screaming while I was being put in the ambulance, but I did not hear them.

Waking up two days later smelling like medicine and BO, the first time anyone in the hospital knew I was conscious was when I asked to take a bath. Then everyone came in, including Patty, and the nurse called the doctor. Everybody was checking me out to see if I could see, hear, talk, move, and acknowledge speech. I kept asking for a bath. I smelled bad! The nurses set me up in a shower with a stool and I stayed in there soaping for a long time. Bad head pain, dizziness… aftershocks of all kinds… one tough old man, evidently.

Dr. Max P. Benzaquen came in and told me all about my disease and fight with the encephalitis, what it had tried to do by conquering the brain and that I did face death. He saved my life. He said a medicine called an antiviral chemotherapy drug used to treat viral infections saved my life. It was used intravenously and stopped the virus from further attack.

It took two weeks at home to recover from the viral attack, but I didn't fully recover. Serious depression set in, and I headed to a recommended psychiatrist, Dr. William Irwin, Jr., who immediately treated me for the depression, questioned me extensively about my life, and told me I had a lot of trauma in my life and a full psychiatric work up was needed because maybe depression was only a symptom of something greater. I didn't understand what he meant, took the medication he gave me, and went my way.

Things were getting anxious for me; I was racking up bills for school and not getting any job bites on my resumes. I kept seeing Dr. Irwin but was beginning to think it was a waste of time and insurance to continue in therapy.

Dr. Irwin diagnosed me with post traumatic stress syndrome, and he said I was bipolar along with serious clinical depression. He explained I had probably been living with these brain dysfunctions for a long time but now was time to get treatment.

PJ AND ELLISVILLE A. A.

On October 19, 1985, in St. Louis, Missouri, one of the busiest child athletes was born. His career highlights included baseball, soccer, karate, basketball, and seven years of football. All sports were played according to the seasons of the year and sometimes ending one sport being played concomitantly during tournament times with another sport. This kid had some energy. In baseball, Patrick played first base and later pitched taking pitching lessons from a professional pitching coach, Carl McKay. Patrick played goalie for his soccer team and played guard in basketball. PJ played football in junior high through varsity for four years in high school, as a Lafayette Lancer in Wildwood, Missouri. Patrick lettered all four years he was playing varsity football and of course he had mixed feelings about always playing the "line".

His athletic career started in 1992 at Jefferson Barrack Park Boys and Girls Club of St. Louis County. There PJ started hitting T-Ball and became a member of a team his father, me, became the manager of because I was the only parent who showed up for the volunteers' meeting. Such luck. We had a team of about twelve players who were mixed boys and girls, and the drills for baseball were taught along with the rules. The little ones caught on fast, and before anyone knew it, we had games going on with other organized teams.

Before long, my kids were hitting "coach-pitch" instead of using the traditional T-Ball stand. I was a pitcher, but I should say I was a line drive ricochet body, getting clobbered by a strong hit back by some seven-year olds really hurt. Too bad coach.

Patrick and I played T-Ball for two years before we moved to Ellisville Athletic Association, in Ellisville, Missouri. We lived in Wildwood, Missouri and chose E.A.A. because of its size, eight ballfields and beauty.

(Side note: Ellisville Athletic Association is a volunteer organized and operated Baseball Park run by an elected set of board of directors. The park is held in trust for the benefit of the residents of the area. There are several employees at the park but the directors are all vol-

unteers and must be elected for their efforts and abilities every year. Considered the best ball park in the area this is a direct result of the work of the volunteer B.O. directors. They have an enrollment of over 1,000 ball players from age five through age eighteen. I was elected a board member and worked for E.A.A. for nine years, as a scheduler, computer set-up operator when the park first started using computers in the office. I did invent and build the PlayBall scheduling system to use at E.A.A. but that's another story.)

PJ registered to play spring ball 1994, at E.A.A. and we were put into the continental division of coach pitch or "machine pitch" level. Again, the park needed parent volunteers to manage and run the teams and found out about my T-Ball coaching experience and latched on to me as team everything including parent coordinator, the most difficult job of all. Parents were normally out of control until your calming voice told them it "was just a game", after that, most parents only lost control if their kid's team lost.

The majority of parents were not anxiety ridden when they came to watch a game, but there were some who lost control quickly and often. These parents I had to embarrass by telling them to either calm down or go home...

even this didn't work with the diehards. I had to come to the rescue of many an umpire during tournament time with some of my parents. And as the kids got older and the competition became more intense, so did the parents. When I was a board member and the umpire coordinator, it was not unusual for me to call the police to help calm some parents down. It always worked when they saw me coming towards them with a cop, who just told them to calm down... Presto, an apology after the game from the offender and usually all was well.

Patrick played spring and fall baseball for six years at E.A.A. and interspersed that with soccer during weekdays of the fall with game conflicts sometimes causing minor inconveniences. We signed up for soccer at St. Alban's parish. They needed volunteers also to man the manager's position, and since it was no big deal for me, I stepped forward. Mike the electrician (I never knew his last name, but he did the electrical work on my father-in-law's house, hence the nickname) ran the soccer organization. Mike did a fair job and he and I only butted heads once over a rain-out he never called me about, when I called him and asked him why he didn't call me about the canceled game, Mike just said, "Hey I've got people over," and then hung up... while we stood in the drizzle twenty miles from home.

One parent came forward and said he'd coach the soccer team if I'd do everything else on the team such as parent and scheduling coordinator. I asked him if he knew kids' soccer, he said yes. I was asking coach Ernie Sprunger if he knew kids' soccer. His daughter lettered varsity, and so did his oldest son and coach Sprunger could teach Pele how to kick a ball. We were the envy of the league with Coach Sprunger.

PJ was a stocky kid like his old man, and he was fairly fast at soccer but had the habit of a budding football player, (he was in football in his last year of soccer), and he hit the opposing soccer ball carrier to steal the ball, sending the opponent to the ground. So, coach put Patrick in as goalie and he was a dang fine goalie, nothing got by him if he could help it. Diving every which way and using head to toe to stop the ball.

Soccer season ended in October, and we signed up for basketball at the Rockwood School District Basketball Association, which was 1,400 kids strong, and Mr. Bill Wagner Director and volunteer selector. He sent me a letter when I registered PJ and wrote a short resume concerning my children's sports experience.

I thought maybe they could use me for Patrick's team, and I could find a parent coach like we had in soccer with coach Sprunger. But noooooo... I became one of seven parent volunteers who Mr. Wagner picked to help him coordinate and run the organization.

Team parity was a problem like it was in all of Patrick's sports organizations. I stepped forward and with computer in hand showed Mr. Wagner how we could use a matrix to even out player's ability with team census and then like they had at Evansville Athletic Association create a model of teams that play one another with player similar skill levels.

The first year we used the system I invented was a huge success, no complaining parents or kids, well, almost none. That first year I was given two teams to manage, an excellent bunch of kids who could play Louisville and a set of kids who needed to sharpen their skills, just to see if my parity system worked. My parity system is still being used.

Mr. Wagner figured that the parity system worked so well he gave me the job of writing the parents handbook for little league basketball, which I did over a two month off season period. Mr. Wagner critiqued the handbook, and it was printed for use and all parents received a copy when they registered. The handbook contains rules of play and manners at games. Also, what the job of officials was and what their calls meant. I was proud of my nineteen-page work of art and I'm sure by now it has been updated, but the crux of the book has to remain the same because the material hasn't changed that much. Rules are rules and good manners should never change.

My next assignment as the volunteer of the year came (that's what I called myself whenever I got tired of being an unpaid helper for the kids) when I set up the holiday tournament. Tournament play was between Christmas Day and New Year's Day. Mr. Wagner laid down the rules of the tournament so things wouldn't get out of hand by the better teams over the learning teams and gave me the keys to the entire school building where the tournaments would take place. I registered about forty-five teams who wanted to play, collected registration money, drew up a matrix model, paired the teams the best I could, hired timekeepers, security, and two weeks later the hired people and officials welcomed the players to a full house fan section.

I never expected so many fans. I mean all games were packed. Funny story - On court one, tournament play had stopped in the middle of a game – the officials did not know how to decide on a call which was important to the game – they claimed only the tournament commissioner could decide on the call – so they thought 'go get Tim, he's the commissionerm isn't he?' – I got tracked down by a kid who exclaims, "Hey they need you at court one right away!" I thought somebody got hurt. I had a clipboard with me thatcontained notes about how to use the alarm lock up when the tournament was over and I hobbled into court one which was packed with probably 200 people and the two teams and three officials (and so quiet you could a hear a mouse fart). All stare at me when one of the officials motions me to center court. They explain 'whatever' but in my mind I'm trying to get over the position I'm in with all this attention on me, and I rule the ball was out of bounds. ALL OF A SUDDEN, THE CROWD ROARS, good cheers, and the officials shake their heads at me in unison as yes, good call… and I was guessing, but it looked out of bounds. Funny story.

Mr. Wagner wanted me to stay on a fourth year as a volunteer, but E.A.A. was where my heart was, and I had some ideas about trying to do more with computers at E.A.A. I had my master's in computer science and wanted to put a voice recognition system together for baseball rainout rescheduling.

AS LIFE CONTINUES

My heart surgery at this time in my life involved the Aortic Valve repair which meant I was on a heart lung machine for 6 plus hours, and the main complication came when my blood sugar spiked during surgery. My surgeon told my wife this was a problem during the operation but came under control. Dr. Welch told my wife this may bring on serious complications with my diabetes sickness in the future.

Going in for heart surgery is truly scary to say the least. I prayed and prayed (I've been a big prayer since the wreck), so that I would make it through this heart operation. You can't help but have imagination take over periods where you think you are surely going to die. The getting naked and putting on the surgical gown is enough to raise anyone's blood pressure. And when the masked surgical people start coming at you to ask questions and administer shots while you're being rolled onto the surgical gurney, is pure fear of the; "it's too late to turn back now!"

They set me in a hallway space with dark windows and white walls with dim lighting and I asked the man who parked my gurney if this hallway was supposed to be ominous looking on purpose?

Once in surgery command, as I called it, the nurse stuck my hand with a needle trying to find a vein, but my skin was so tough and my veins so constricted due to my muscular dystrophy, the nurse had a hard time trying to locate a vein. She did have my hand pretty well bloody before she was done. Over my face went the plastic breathing mask and I was told to count to 100 and I went out like a light.

The nurse was right, the next instant I was waking up in a room full of machines making every noise possible and with every noise came a blinking light. Tubes everywhere. I had tubes down my throat, down my nose, up my private part, blood lines and bottles of every concoction possible hanging above me. A nurse looked at me and I looked back at her, and she yelled, some medical code and my room number I guess, because I had no idea where I was. And then came a swift rush of two or three other

people in gowns, and one fella in a mask yet who introduced himself as Dr. Allworth. He told me I came through
the operation just fine and there were a few things we
would have to go over when I was back on my feet. Feet?

I started thinking about where I left my artificial leg
which I was wearing the day before. I'd forgotten where
I'd left it. My wife later told me it was safe under the desk
of one of her coworkers at the hospital for safe keeping
.and the nurses were all breaking the stress by knowing it
was safe and sound. Here I am, barely alive and butchered
up like an old hog, worrying about my damn artificial leg,
as if somebody would steal it or if someone found it they
wouldn't turn it in to security.

Well I had a lot planned as far as schooling was concerned. I aimed for my PHD or Dr. of Management in
business. But the heart surgery derailed all of that plan-
ning. I came out of surgery with tremendous pain in my
rheumatoid arthritic hands. I'd had arthritis for many
years but at a low level of deformity and pain, but it seems
like what Doctor Kelly, my General Practitioner said was
true, this could be a result of the six plus hours on the
heart lung machine. Doctor Kelly gave me medication for
the arthritis and my newly develop migraines while direct-
ing me to a specialist. I had too many doctors, so I stuck

it out with my medicine and never went to see the specialist. To this day I'll get a migraine and of course there is no cure for twisted fingers of arthritis, but I manage.

One after effect of the surgery which two doctors concluded could be the direct result of the heart lung machine was the making worse my depression. Doctor Irving did not want to commit to saying the operation was a direct result, but he told me more and more research by qualified people have shown there is a correlation. All it meant for me was why I now was feeling so miserable? Doctor Irving then as now keeps me on medication that seems to work, I see Doctor Irving every three months and have been for 15 years and we stay on top of the medicines I need.

I have had sleep apnea for 20 years and must sleep with a assistant breathing CPAP machine and mask. Those times I've forgotten my machine and mask and stayed overnight somewhere is misery in the making. My rough breathing causes the wiring Dr. Allworth wired my breastbone back together with to move and rub together.... that'll wake you up, Doctor Susan Deslodge examined me, tested the movement and said it was okay. But a reminder to me that I am simply wired together.

I could not teach because of my hearing, even an expensive hearing aid didn't help. I was out of school and dreams of a terminal degree were gone. I kept busy watching grandchildren and polishing my programming skills especially my voice to voice systems. I want computers to be able to ask us free-thought artificial intelligence questions and then be able to determine how to perform a routine according to the answer given by the person, or other computer. Easy to think through, but difficult to code, eh! (my Mother was Canadian).

DAMMIT

I have terrible bottom teeth, my top teeth were partially removed during the wreck, but my bottom teeth have been taken out two by two by an oral surgeon. Two by two was my idea because I hate dentistry. The sound of the cracking and splintering of bone, the warm feeling of blood running down your throat, and in case you have to have a big tooth excavated, the good old saw. So I told my favorite Dentist (a true Irish blessing to him, Doctor St. John, only two at a time. We are taking teeth out to this day…

I went thru tests to discover if three spots on my face and a mole on my arm were cancerous. Dr Sanmina removed the facial blemishes with a quick surgery and thee lab sent back a benign report on the three tissue samples.

Dr Wolff took a biopsy of the arm mole and it also came back negative. I was happy and lucky both.

Wearing my leg now is more and more of a strain. I kept falling down, and steps were especially dangerous… I fell down our bottom level steps from about halfway up and hit the back of my head on the uncarpeted concrete floor. To the hospital I went when my wife, a registered nurse who figured I had a concussion. At the hospital I was given an MRI, and nothing showed up… I had to stay there six hours to be observed.

I fell down the same set of steps about two weeks later and this time I was given a CAT scan… still nothing to worry about. When I'd fall my body somehow would go into a restrictive posture because I never came up with anything more than a head injury, no broken collar bones, arms, leg, foot, hands, but plenty of bruises and scrapes. The final time on the artificial leg came when I went to get a haircut, left the building and proceed to lose my balance in the street. I was crossing the street when down I went on the side of my face I landed and on my left elbow. Blood started coming from my nose and my elbow and here I was trying to lift my busted self-back up. I drew a crowd and a couple of folks helped me up while someone gave me a towel.

I managed to get to my Van before I started my cussing, looked in the mirror and started to laugh in the most ironic way... how could a guy just go to get a haircut and go home with a shirt smeared with blood? When I got home, my wife stopped what she was doing and yelled, "What happened to you?!" I got cleaned up, took the damn leg off and never put it on again.

Being in a wheelchair is no fun. At least with an artificial leg your hands are free unless you have to use a cane, but even then, you have one hand free, but not with a wheelchair. Getting on a chair is a matter of engineering. Try getting on a chair with only one bad leg the other leg missing, yeah, it's not easy. I adapted to my chairs but seemed to tear them up faster than I could get them repaired. I went everywhere with my chair and drove anywhere I had to go. I had to do what I have called is "scooching" to get around the house when I wasn't in my chair. Scooching is a matter of being in a sitting position and moving along by arm and shoulder power. Fairly efficient manner of getting along, go ahead try it...

Well scooching does have its drawbacks, and the biggest one is if you wear a brace, which I still had to do when I was driving. Well lo and behold the driving and brace gave me a small infectious sore on the lateral side of my left ankle. One you could not see, and you did not know was there until it stated to hurt like a cyst, which I'm always getting.

I show my wife, she says we need to se Dr. Kelly, he sends me to a Podiatrist who immediately informs me that this is a bigger problem than I realize because the infection has gone inside the foot and attached itself to the bones. Off to St. Mary's I go.

At the ER my wife had to get one of her security employee friends to help me get from the Caravan to a hospital gurney. I'm in the emergency room eight hours before an attending physician sent me to a floor and a room. I'm just settling in when a surgeon comes into the room and sits down next to me, asks my wife to stay in the room and states that the X-Rays taken in the emergency room indicate that the bone infection is quite widespread and intense.

The doctor continued that what we have is a case of osteomyelitis, which was getting ready to spread thru the body and infect other organs. The only way to stop the infection was to amputate the left leg immediately, such as tomorrow morning. The doctor stress there was no time to waste because the infection was the type that could be further along then just X-Rays could indicate.

Then the doctor indicated he would like an answer, and I told him I would like a second opinion, he agreed, but told me to notify the nurse by 4pm what my decision was going to be.

Dr. Brickhouse, a podiatrist, came in and examined my foot, didn't say much but told me he was sending me out for some more test. Well after more tests than a few, Dr. Brickhouse comes in that evening and tells me there is a slim chance he can save the leg with surgery and with long term antibiotic therapy can clear up the infection.

Eight days more in the hospital, and four months in a Rehabilitation center, with a total of nine months of no weight bearing on my only leg.

One morning in the rehabilitation center I woke up with my right arm twice as big as my left arm and red, really red. Well one look by the nurse and the doctor who was called ordered me to the hospital immediately, he told me my fluid PIC line to my heart had broken inside me somewhere and if it had broken in my heart I would need immediate heart surgery to retrieve it.

When I got to the hospital, they took me to a pre-operation room, pulled out what was still in my arm as far as a pic line was concerned and measured it. The doctor on duty and the pic line nurse specialist decided the line had not broken but had become infected and caused a blood clot and infection…eight more days in the hospital, and two pic lines inserted in the neck tissue via the Radiology Department. A lot of pain, especially when the doctor has to do it twice in tender neck tissue.

It was a fun day when thy removed my pic lines weeks later, and the blood clot was no longer a scare.

I'm here today with a still good scooching leg. The most frustrating part of the whole thing was when my beloved Uncle Tony died while I was laid up, and there was just no way I could go to the funeral to say good bye. I mean my bandages were changed three times a day because the doctor left a hole in my ankle for drainage and man did it work, I changed a bath towel of fluid twice a day, I couldn't put my foot down on the floor even to go from bed to wheelchair, how was I supposed to use a public bathroom? Well I only bring this up because not everyone forgave me for not showing up.

I visit Doctor Brickhouse every six weeks or so to let him check the foot because I've been told the infection could return.

In fact, I see a different doctor almost every month for everything from my psoriasis, my headaches, my cardiologist, my shrink and all for preventative help. Every now and then I see a doctor for an actual immediate ailment, butt that's life and I still enjoy mine because I've learned to overcome sickness and trauma and reclaim my life.

Then comes February 9, 2019 and I wake up in the middle of the night with great pain trying to urinate and nothing comes out but blood. I yelled for my wife to help me, she's an RN, and she comes running from her bedroom to mine and notices in my underwear and urinal that I normally urinate in that there is nothing but blood so she immediately called 911 and the paramedics arrived. The paramedics examined me and discovered that sure enough I'm urinating blood and they have to get me from the second floor down to the gurney on the first floor so what they do is a make a towel lift and drag me down the steps put me on the gurney and put me in the ambulance and take me to St. John's Mercy Hospital where I go into the emergency room and immediately I'm surrendered to the doctors on duty.

The first thing the doctors do is examine me and discover that a portion of what I'm relieving is urine and blood they run a few tests see if my bladder is bursting or if I have any sort of growth in the bladder. The doctors run a ultrasound test and then they decide to go ahead and take the blood clots out of the urethra which is excruciatingly painful and takes over an hour. Each blood clot is picked out by forceps and each one causes me to grimace in pain and yell out, there are many blood clots that had to be removed and I'm given no pain killer. Then I'm fitted with a Foley catheter.

I'm exhausted from the pain and misery that I just went through, and I'm sent to a room in the near ICU unit till the doctors can figure out what went wrong and what is wrong with me.

My wife was as shocked as I was with what just happened because neither one of us saw it coming, I had not felt well for several days but didn't feel anything in my bladder that would indicate something was wrong down there. She stayed with me for several hours while I was getting accustomed to the hospital room and then she went home, by now it was late at night.

I'd doze off or pass out and no sooner would that happen then somebody from the nursing staff would wake and wake me up to draw blood or blood test measurement would take place. These interruptions happened every day and night every night I was at the hospital. It's a matter of standard operating procedure at hospitals when they don't know what's wrong with you.

I was in the DICU unit for nine days when it was discovered by my wife during a routine cardiogram test that my heart was not beating in sync. My wife alerted the nurse and the cardiology clerk to notify the doctor that there was a problem, they did so and the doctor paid attention to the fact that my heart was not beating properly, there was a skip in the beat.

The next day I was brought to the cardiology room and was given a full examination and it was declared that I had to have an electroshock at the heart to get it properly beat again.

This had nothing to do with my bladder problem but it was a problem of great magnitude in and of itself. So up to the surgical unit in the cardiology lab I went, and a camera was stuck down my throat after I was anesthetized. To search for blood clots because the electroshock would not be allowed if there are blood clots in my lungs because this could be dangerous. There were not any blood clots found so the electroshock was administered, and my heart was brought back into sync and beating properly, and I was okay. Something so important as your heart beating irregularly being discovered during a routine test by your better than intelligent wife surely is a blessing.

After nine days of hospitalization and assorted medications with more than many tests, I was considered good enough to leave the main hospital and transfer to St John's Mercy Rehabilitation Hospitalization Hospital.

ADDENDUM

I was operated on January 25th, 2022, for a 'look see' into my bladder with a small camera. The doctor examined the inside of the bladder for any foreign bodies or growths that could spell trouble, like cancer. But lucky for me nothing was discovered, and the procedure was soon ended. Or so I thought.

Sometime and somewhere during the bladder examination procedure tainted blood with germ bacteria entered my system, and the germ immediately began growing. Ten days after the procedure I became sick with dizzy spells and I asked Patty to get me to the hospital. She called 911 and an ambulance took me to St. John's Mercy Hospital where I immediately was plugged into antibiotics. The staff at the emergency wanted to know if the slight gray color was my natural complexion. I was one seriously sick old man.

I stayed at Mercy Hospital for nine days taking in all sorts of medications and pharmaceuticals to counter act the germ I was attacked by and had to regain my strength, no easy task. There is not a lot to tell about my treatment except for the constant drip of thee IV's I was taking in and the shots now and then, secondary to my five diabetic shots a day. I had to lay in bed and every now and then a therapist would help me exercise, and eventually get back into my wheelchair.

Blood test withdrawal shots riddled my arms to the point of making my forearms the colors of black and blue. Since the germ was in my blood the doctors kept a sharp eye on whether it was growing or receding.

After nine days of intensive medicine therapy I was given the all clear to transfer to the Mercy Rehabilitation Hospital. Where I began a routine of strength training and wheelchair usage. Fourteen days of weight training using dumbbells, barbells, machines, and whatever else a man in a wheelchair could use to build strength.

Life continued on track for me for many months until I awoke on March 3rd, 2023. When I came to at about 6 am with the chills and a sneeze and a cough combo. Then my wife woke up to all my commotion, felt my forehead and got out the family thermometer and shoved it under my tongue. She exclaimed, "You've got a fever, buddy, what's wrong with you now?"

My wife, the registered nurse had her thoughts that a cold with a fever coming on so quickly during this time may indicate testing for Covid-19. Using a hospital qualified testing system supplied from the U S Government, my wife tested me and found out I was a positive for having Covid-19.

As I began my six weeks of guaranteed living and Paxlovid medication, my mask wearing became second nature within a short time. The headache pain and the coughing and sneezing were always with me and I soon lost my voice, but good Dr. Gage told me as I had a caring nurse at home and a visiting nurse contracted to come to the house each week for my other ailments, there was no need for me to be hospitalize yet. Dr. K. Gage told me I also had had two Covid-19 inoculations and a booster shot within the last 18 months and this would help my fight against the Covid virus.

I mainly stayed in bed and suffered and sometimes would write at my desk whenever possible; I'm writing two science fiction novels now at the same time, trying to keep the stories separate and individualized as possible. One story about mankind's beginnings through the lens of anthropology, and the other story regarding human exploration of extraterrestrials. Both novels are more than half way done as of this writing, but my Covid sickness is slowing me down quite a bit.

But alas, after many weeks of sickness, coughing, and laryngitis, sneezing, aches and pains, I came out of the spell of the virus that so harshly knocked me down. I am back to my routine of getting myself out of bed and into my wheelchair, then going to my stair climber, getting myself to my down stair's wheelchair, and then making my moring protein shakes with my Metamucil, and after a brief e-mail check, I start my 8 lb to 12 lb lifting exercises. A necessity to stay strong if you wish to wrestle wheelchairs and a stair climber down and then back up every day.

With my daily prayers and an irresistible will to live I keep pushing the envelope so to speak. I look to God through my sight upon Jesus, and I'm always trying to keep myself in shape, no matter my age, so my next "knock down" won't be such a surprise for a sinner such as myself. God Bless You !

THE ST. JOHN'S MERCY
REHABILITATION HOSPITAL

I finally found a place where I could heal up and even improve my body situation, St. John's Mercy Rehabilitation Hospital. The staff of this hospital consisted of doctors, nurses, occupational therapist, physical therapist, and counselors. Patients came from St. John's main hospital and were to of course rehabilitate for two weeks while here. Some folks were in serious condition, such as stroke survivors and others were like me just laid up enough for medicine intake that did not allow for the freedom of going home.

The only pain medication I took was Tylenol every six hours or so, and an occasional pain pill of the hydrocodone type. But these pills would block you up tighter than concrete while making you want to go at the same time. Bad news for me!

Anyway, it's about this time I decide I wasn't to try and walk again and what better place to try then when you get out of the rehabilitation hospital after two weeks of basic muscle and balance training.

I go to Prosthetic and Orthotic Design and get measured for a new prothesis. The measuring and casting take over an hour and I come away surprised that I've gained so much weight. So immediately my wife puts me on a diet and Mr. Carte, my prosthetist tells me my limb will be mock=up stage fitting ready in about four weeks.

Well four weeks flies by and I'm introduced to my new limb. I get it on but can not walk on it outside of the parallel bars or a walker without hitting my old friend and nemesis gravity, but it sure beats sitting in a wheelchair. I take the limb home unfinished to practice on with a walker. Practice time is limited because we live in a small house and everything I need or am responsible for comes through on the wheelchair.

And so, I go on the long road of learning to walk again on my newest artificial leg with the hope of getting back on my feet..

A hope filled life is not one that avoids pain, a hopeful life is when you are knocked down many times and get back on your feet many times more. A hopeful life is what brings you back. The Rehabilitation Hospital taught us through training that you only succeed via persistence.

I have been to two other area rehabilitation hospitals and spent as may as three months at one institution, and they cannot compare to Mercy Hospital. Comparing tools for the patients to use for strength training and muscle work, and cleanliness is a plus for Mercy.

Suffering in life can uncover untold depths of character and unknown strength for service. People who go through life unscathed by sorrow and untouched by pain tend to be shallow in their perspectives on life. Suffering, on the other hand, tends to plow up the surface of people's lives and uncover the deaths that provide greater strength of purpose and accomplishment. Only deeply plowed earth can you a bountiful harvest.

...Billy Graham

TOPICS THAT I LEARNED
TO GUIDE MY LIFE

For Further Study by my Grandchildren

Emotional intelligence (EI) is the capability of individuals to recognize their own, and other people's emotions, to discern between different feelings and label them appropriately, to use emotional information to guide thinking and behavior, and to manage and/or adjust emotions to adapt environments or achieve one's goals.

Although the term first appears in a book of that title, written by the author, psychologist, Daniel Goleman. It encompasses behavioral dispositions and self-perceived abilities and is measured through an individual's ability to process emotional information and use it to navigate the social environment.

Studies have shown that people with high EI have greater mental health, job performance, and leadership skills although no causal relationships have been shown and such findings are likely to be attributable to general intelligence and specific personality traits. Leadership and managerial performance is non-significant when ability and personality are controlled for, and that general intelligence correlates very closely with leadership.

Review finds that, in most studies, poor research methodology has exaggerated the significance of EI.

Emotional intelligence can be defined as the ability to monitor one's own and other people's emotions, to discriminate between different emotions and label them appropriately and to use emotional information to guide thinking and behavior. Emotional intelligence also reflects abilities to join intelligence, empathy and emotions to enhance thought and understanding of interpersonal dynamics toward people, environment and circumstances one encounters in daily life.

PERSONAL EFFICACY

Personal effectiveness, is the extent or strength of one's belief in one's own ability to complete tasks and reach goals. Psychologists have studied self-efficacy from several perspectives, noting various paths in the development of self-efficacy; the dynamics of self-efficacy, and lack thereof, in many different settings; interactions between self-efficacy and self-concept; and habits of attribution that contribute to, or detract from, self-efficacy.

Self-efficacy affects every area of human endeavor. By determining the beliefs, a person holds regarding his or her power to affect situations, it strongly influences both the power a person actually has to face challenges competently and the choices a person is most likely to make. These effects are particularly apparent, and compelling, with regard to behaviors affecting health.

Self-efficacy is one's belief in one's ability to succeed in specific situations or accomplish a task. One's sense of self-efficacy can play a major role in how one approaches goals, tasks, and challenges. Self-efficacy represents the personal perception of external social factors.

People with high self-efficacy—that is, those who believe they can perform well—are more likely to view difficult tasks as something to be mastered rather than something to be avoided.

Social learning depends on how individuals either succeed or fail at dynamic interactions within groups, and promotes the development of individual emotional and practical skills as well as accurate perception of self and acceptance of others. According to this theory, people learn from one another through observation,

**According to psychologists ,"Children cannot be fooled by empty praise and condescending encouragement. They may have to accept artificial bolstering of their self-esteem in lieu of something better, but what I call their accruing ego identity gains real strength only from wholehearted and consistent recognition of real accomplishment, that is, achievement that has meaning in their culture."

1. Modeling, or "vicarious experience" – Modeling is experienced as, "If they can do it, I can do it as well". When we see someone succeeding, our own self-efficacy increases; where we see people failing, our self-efficacy decreases. This process is most effectual when we see ourselves as similar to the model. Although not as influential as direct

experience, modeling is particularly useful for people who are particularly unsure of themselves.

2. Social persuasion – Social persuasion generally manifests as direct encouragement or discouragement from another person. Discouragement is generally more effective at decreasing a person's self-efficacy than encouragement is at increasing it.

3. Physiological factors – In stressful situations, people commonly exhibit signs of distress: shakes, aches and pains, fatigue, fear, nausea, etc. Perceptions of these responses in oneself can markedly alter self-efficacy. Getting 'butterflies in the stomach' before public speaking will be interpreted by someone with low self-efficacy as a sign of inability, thus decreasing self-efficacy further, where high self-efficacy would lead to interpreting such physiological signs as normal and unrelated to ability. It is one's belief in the implications of physiological response that alters self-efficacy, rather than the physiological response itself.

MAJOR DEPRESSIVE DISORDER

And possibilities for Major depressive disorder (MDD), also known simply as depression, is a mental disorder characterized by at least two weeks of low mood that is present across most situations. It is often accompanied by low self-esteem, loss of interest in normally enjoyable activities, low energy, and pain without a clear cause. People may also occasionally have false beliefs or see or hear things that others cannot. https://en.wikipedia.org/ wiki/Major_depressive_disorder - cite_note-NIH2016-1 Some people have periods of depression separated by years in which they are normal while others nearly always have symptoms present.[2] Major depressive disorder can negatively affects a person's personal, work, or school life, as well as sleeping, eating habits, and general health.[

The cause is believed to be a combination of genetic, environmental, and psychological factors. Risk factors include a family history of the condition, major life changes, certain medications, chronic health problems, and substance abuse. About 40% of the risk appears to be related to genetics. The diagnosis of major depressive disorder is based on the person's reported experiences and a mental status examination. There is no laboratory test for major depression.[2] Testing, however, may be done to rule out physical conditions that can cause similar symptoms. Major depression should be differentiated from sadness which is a normal part of life and is less severe.

***The United States Preventive Services Task Force (USPSTF) recommends screening for depression among those over the age 12.

Typically, people are treated with counselling and antidepressant medication. Medication appears to be effective, but the effect may only be significant in the most severely depressed. Types of counselling used include cognitive behavioral therapy (CBT) and interpersonal therapy.https://en.wikipedia.org/wiki/Major_depressive_disorder - cite_note-NIH2016-1 If other measures are not effective electroconvulsive therapy (ECT) may be tried. Hospitalization may be necessary in cases with a risk of harm to self and may occasionally occur against a person's wishes. Depression significantly affects a person's family and personal relationship work or school life, sleeping and eating habits, and general health.

Feelings of worthlessness, inappropriate guilt or regret, helplessness, hopelessness, and self-hatred. In severe cases, depressed people may have symptoms of psychosis.

These symptoms include delusions or, less commonly, hallucinations, usually unpleasant. Other symptoms of depression include poor concentration and memory (especially in those with melancholic or psychotic features), withdrawal from social situations and activities, reduced sex drive, irritability, and thoughts of death or suicide. Insomnia is common among the depressed. In the typical pattern, a person wakes very early and cannot get back to sleep.

Depressed children may often display an irritable mood rather than a depressed mood, varying symptoms depending on age and situation. Most lose interest in school and show a decline in academic performance. They may be described as clingy, demanding, dependent, or insecure. Diagnosis may be delayed or missed when symptoms are interpreted as normal moodiness. Around a third of individuals diagnosed with ADHD develop comorbid depression.

CAUSE

Child abuse, either physical, sexual or psychological are all risk factors for depression, among other psychiatric issues that co-occur such as anxiety and drug abuse. Childhood trauma also correlates with severity of depression, lack of response to treatment and length of illness. However, some are more susceptible to developing mental illness such as depression after trauma, and various genes have been suggested to control susceptibility. It is an inherited factor according to my doctors.

ACKNOWLEDGEMENTS

I wish to thank God our Father, Jesus, and the Bible.

I want to thank my wife Miss Patty for everything she has done for me concerning my life and this book, such as editing it for spelling errors.

My sister Bridget Fay was a big help reading the rough drafts and helping me with this book, and I want to thank Uncle John Hartman also.

Thank you, Mary Anne, for my grandchildren, and, oh, thank you also Vince Sweeney!

Thanks, Patrick, for your help, your smarts keep amazing me with your studies of the human mind and child behavior.

Thank you, Uncle John McGuirk, for the beautiful illustrations and thank you Aunt Norma for finding the hilarity in the parts of this book that were written to be humorous.

Thank you to Nicole and her team at Dorrance Publishing Co.

Suffering in life can uncover untold depths of character and unknown strength for service. People who go through life unscathed by sorrow and untouched by pain tend to be shallow in their perspectives on life. Suffering, on the other hand, tends to plow up the surface of people's lives and uncover the depths that provide greater strength of purpose and accomplishment. Only deeply plowed earth can you a bountiful harvest gain.

Billy Graham

Printed in the USA
CPSIA information can be obtained
at www.ICGtesting.com
CBHW061115240724
12037CB00025B/916

9 798889 251187